VOICES OF MAGIC

Cover Art, "Close to Home" painting on silk
Copyright © 2019 Patricia Walkar

"Iris" pencil sketch
Copyright © 2021 Patricia Walkar

The Lazaris Material™ is © NPN Publishing, Inc.
Produced exclusively by Concept: Synergy
PO Box 1789
Sonoma, CA 95476
407-401-8990
www.Lazaris.com
conceptsynergy@Lazaris.com

MMW Publishing
magicianbook1@gmail.com
Providence, RI

VOICES OF MAGIC

Reality Creating,
Healing & Love
in a Modern World

Edited by

Mary Woodhouse

To everyone who believes in magic, or wants to.

CONTENTS

COVER ART

"Close to Home"

*Belonging is a choice
made by an open heart.*

"Close to Home" is a painting on silk by Patricia Walkar. The bouquet combines flowers from her and her neighbor's garden, celebrating Patricia and her neighbor's warm friendship.

Artist's Statement

I am primarily a self-taught artist. Drawing has always been a natural form of expression for me, and my fascination with people's faces led me in the direction of portrait making.

Some years ago my focus shifted to representing my own inner images and privately held voices. My paintings became rich blends of color and design that began to reflect a journey of the spirit.

The result has been a dance with beauty that has brought joy and healing to me and those who share my art.

Patricia Walkar

FOREWORD

Voices of Magic

The carpet pile had a soft musty smell, and it was rough against my cheek. It was 2:30 in the morning and I was lying on the living room floor watching two Panasonic cassette players. One playing. The other recording. I was waiting for the sides to finish so that I could flip the two cassettes over, hit play and record, and get back to bed.

That was forty-six years ago and only several months after Lazaris had begun channeling through me. The whole channeling experience was so new and still unsettling. I didn't fully understand what was happening to me. Or why.

While the duplication was happening, I listened. What else could I do? I don't remember what Lazaris was saying, and back then I didn't understand what he was talking about. Half asleep, half awake, I waited. I listened.

It wasn't a voice I heard in words. Yet, it was a voice that rippled through me and brought tears to my eyes. Almost overwhelmed, I sat up wide-eyed and wide awake. Since I had been channeling for several months, I had heard Lazaris' voice many times. This wasn't the first time, but this particular moment, at 2:30 in the morning, while I was lying on the living room floor, was unique; it was magic.

In that moment, I knew. I felt the intensity of knowing like nothing I had ever experienced before. Between the words, I suppose, or maybe beyond them, I felt Lazaris' immense love for humankind and his intense compassion for all of us. His commitment.

I knew that that intensity was not mine. That depth of compassion was not mine. That love and compassion were someone else's. It was a voice of love that was deafening without making a single sound, and it was Lazaris' voice, not mine.

That was a defining moment, my moment of absolute knowing that I was channeling a non-physical entity that was not me, not even a part of me. In that moment, I realized I didn't need anyone's permission or approval; I knew what and who Lazaris was. I also caught a glimpse of who I was. I felt the magic of knowing, and I felt honored.

I have had several defining moments in my life. That early morning on the living room floor was a moment with a voice of magic that changed me and my life. Forever.

We all have had our own defining moments, moments that are spontaneous and wondrous—ecstatic moments of joy with a sense of peace. Such moments change our lives. Such moments are rich with mystery, and they are shimmering with magic. In those moments, we are touched by the voices of magic and our soul understands. In those enchanted moments, somehow, we can be changed.

This book, *Voices of Magic*, is a compilation of stories of such moments. Each one different. Each one unique. Each one a defining moment of magic and of love. As I read the stories, some made me laugh, others gave me goose bumps of truth, and some brought tears. Each storyteller touched my soul with their story of magic and of its voice. I was moved by the compassion and caring and by the vulnerability woven into each story. Each story and its teller have inspired me to own my magic more fully and to value and honor that I am a magician, a masterful one. These voices of magic help me sharpen and hone my craft. *Voices of Magic* will lift you, and I think you can become more.

Maybe you will read this book in a linear fashion, or maybe you will jump around from front to back and from story to story. However you choose to read *Voices of Magic*, let it be magical. Perhaps you will remember your defining moments and the ones that are alive with the voices of magic for you.

Jach Pursel
Channel for Lazaris
August 2021

PREFACE

A conversation in the Friends of Lazaris private Facebook group inspired the idea to compile this anthology. We were discussing future generations, or anticipated lack of people like us, who have developed a skill and rapport with metaphysics by working with Lazaris.

To our dear reader, who may not be familiar, Lazaris is a non-physical entity, who has been channeling spiritual growth teachings through Jach Pursel since 1974. Concept: Synergy is the company that publishes the Lazaris Material, available on their website, www.lazaris.com. They also host a vibrant online community different from the FB group mentioned above.

Lazaris calls those of us who work with him "magicians." According to his teachings, magic is the act of changing reality in accordance and compliance with one's love and will. Love is what it's all about, and love is truly a many-splendored thing. Love offers a lifetime of exploration, a journey of wondrous self-discovery and creativity.

Lazaris has said many times that they come as a friend, and that's why we often call ourselves friends of Lazaris. Lazaris uses the pronouns "we," "us," and some people refer to Lazaris as "they," "them," and others as "he," or "him." Lazaris' choice of the plural form stems from the vastness of their identity as an entity, which hasn't taken human form, and encompasses all gender energies.

During that Facebook group dialogue, it dawned on me there have been decades of fascinating conversations in private online places. Still, as community members, we have never shared our experiences in an easily accessible, public way, where our stories are the main focus. We've kept ourselves veiled over the past forty-plus years. This invisibility has largely been a protective, intimate privacy that has allowed a multitude of conversations and revelations. Yes, there have been deep conversations about meditative experiences, spiritual concepts, or growth processes, etc.. But people also conversed about TV shows, books, movies, gardening, and the like. Revelations could be personal and spiritual, or, I can say, it was a revelation to me, once upon a time, that magicians are just as varied as anyone else in the rest of the world when it comes to politics or medical beliefs or the interpretation of the day's news. We sometimes face the same challenges as the rest of society does with communication and civility.

Within the private groups, we might share and ask for help with celebrating personal triumphs or healing personal challenges around health, family, work, or any aspect of life. We might work together meditatively to do healing magic for a crisis in the world. We are different from other people in how we view, create, and handle the experiences in living life.

But our longtime privacy also resulted in the fact that our voices and experiences are largely missing from the publicly available material associated with Lazaris. It also occurred to me how helpful it would be to a newcomer to see how individuals approach working with specific recordings, or how they weave together spiritual concepts into their own lives.

So, in the FB group, I broached the old-fashioned idea of creating a book, an anthology of personal stories about working with the Lazaris Material. I hoped someone among the talented, accomplished membership would step up and take off with it. When no one did, but there was excitement and support, I shifted my focus. I recalled this well-known advice: if there is a book you want to read, but it doesn't exist, write it! Another motivation was my happy memories of growing up in a small town and church, where fun community activities were never-ending in their velocity and variety. Why not create this book to get to know a few people better and have fun? Like publishing a church cookbook or putting on a church show?

Two early enthusiastic supporters and magical co-creators joined in. We met a few times on Zoom, with almost breathless excitement. We also worked some magic with one leading an enchanting co-creation meditation of her design. We met in February 2020, before the COVID-19 pandemic was even a thought in our awareness. We were new to Zoom. Odd video angles and awkward fumbling permeated our calls, along with our high spirits. We had only been acquaintances, now connecting to create something new and tangible. We cohesively formed the idea and communicated a better-envisioned project to our friends in the big FB and other groups. When the pandemic forced me to work from home, eliminating my daily commute, I suddenly found myself with a significant amount of extra time to focus on the project.

During this frightening, tragic pandemic, the book project became a much-needed bright spot, with many appreciated moments of connecting with others. We held a few Q&A Zoom socials to recruit writers or used personal messaging and emailing to ask people who showed interest to join. We all had more time and motivation to connect with magicians on Zoom. Without our shared, homebound, isolated state, we may not have found time in our busy lives to spend an hour together on a Tuesday or Wednesday evening.

Many community members came and went, exploring the possibilities, participating for a while, but eventually bowing out. Another intention for the project was for everyone to have the opportunity to get to know each other by creating something together. Many magicians already knew each other and are good friends, but many of us have only been acquaintances these many years. This project offered a unique activity within our community to deepen our relationships.

As a group, we had our fits and starts, ups and downs, developing an approach as we went. Early on, someone shared that classmates in her writing class would read pieces aloud to each other for feedback. So, we decided to try that. A few of our enthusiastic participants dove into their writing immediately and were able to share first drafts right away. Their efforts gave us a solid kick-start.

It took courage to be the first to share their stories in a Zoom read-aloud session. We have a phrase from Lazaris: "There is magic in the telling." We all experienced that magic. Read-aloud Zoom meetings became a wondrous, foundational aspect of developing our individual stories within a community activity. Face to face from around the world and hearing the personal experiences of people like us, who approach life from a spiritual perspective, was inspiring, even thrilling. We were getting to know each other, inspiring each other, and becoming writing pals.

This small band of nineteen magician authors represents various ages, writing experience levels, backgrounds, and geographies. Our stories are personal and true stories of reality creating, healing, and love. Stories of triumph; of encountering worlds of other; of working magic; of intimate conversations; of immersion in concepts and processes; of expanded consciousness; of persistence and perseverance; of miraculous, meaningful happenings; of many successes, as well as challenges. What is magic in a modern world? We reveal to you just a sliver of what it looks like in our lives.

Recruiting enough writers and stories was the major challenge for the project. Participants called out to more folks as months passed, and more fantastic magicians joined our group. With concerted effort, our first drafts eventually became second drafts. A small volunteer team offered comments and encouragement to writers on ways to develop their stories, or pals sent new drafts and made comments furiously back and forth by email.

To transform our second drafts into final pieces, another person suggested we use Grammarly, and so we gave it a try, with success. A bunch of us worked individually with writers, often on Zoom, to review Grammarly suggestions, implement the author's choices, and move the stories closer to a final form. Working together from read-alouds through draft writing and Grammarly sessions helped us get to know each other and gave the project its community feel.

The core volunteer group focused on the cover design, which features artwork offered by Patricia Walkar, a talented artist, who contributed to the project in many ways from start to finish. We chose her painting on silk of a bouquet of flowers, called "Close to Home." Flowers hold a special meaning to magicians. Their beauty is a great gift, deeply enjoyed. A well-loved meditation for self-forgiveness involves imagery of gathering a bouquet of flowers while walking through a valley filled with fields and fields of colorful blooms as part of the overall process.

We were thrilled when Jach Pursel found the project interesting and agreed to write the foreword. His interest alone was encouraging and made a difference in a subtle but meaningful way as we progressed.

From the initial idea to publishing, the entire process took about two years. There was a steep learning curve. This endeavor is essentially a recreational community writing project run by an amateur. How to write a call for submissions? How to contribute our best possible writing quality? How to keep things moving, organized, and true to the initial vision, while encouraging community involvement? What is an author's agreement? What are the publishing options and costs? What are the components of a good cover design? Luckily, writing and self-publishing are well-worn paths. Along with our own efforts, we were able to engage much-needed professionals to help. And work more than a little magic together, of course.

Mary Woodhouse
Editor

PROLOGUE

Magic Indeed!

Magic Indeed! A subject near and dear to my heart.
Does magic work? What is magic anyway?
How do you "do" magic?

I am a Magician. I create reality in accordance with my will and imagination. How is that, you say? Yes, I have many techniques and teachers. Merlin is my number one along with his entourage of knights and ladies. Lazaris is my friend, God/Goddess/All That Is are my co-creators, mystical maps are my guideposts.

What?!? Knights and ladies? Arthur? Merlin and maps?
Are you nuts?

Well, have you ever heard of your Imagination?
Have you ever used it to create Reality?
Have you imagined a Dream Vacation, a Dream House, a Dream Recipe?

Have you desired it so much that you could taste it, hear it, smell it, touch it, see it?
Have you expected that this could/would happen for you?

Then you, too, are a Magician!

Perhaps what's missing is the Consciousness, being consciously aware that you are using Desire, Imagination and Expectation to create your Reality.

Go ahead. Have at it.

And while you are at it, sprinkle a little Fairie Dust along the way. You never know what might happen!

Pamela Dickson

How I Met My Higher Self

Janis Rosen

I found Lazaris in 1989, a few years after the death of my mom, who I cared for during her final stages of cancer, and my grandmother, with whom I was very close. Shortly after their deaths, I read a paragraph in a new age book, where the author mentioned in passing something called the Higher Self.

That phrase, "Higher Self," struck a chord in me and set off a deep longing to find my HS! Though I searched over the years, I couldn't find any other references to the HS. I didn't really know what I was searching for or where to actually find them. I didn't even know if I would recognize it, if I found it. But I started calling for my HS.

One day, I walked into a new age bookstore, that had opened in my city. I wandered around the store, exploring and browsing among the books and things. Eventually, I reached the back of the store. And there, spread along the whole back wall, was an entire library of Lazaris videos and audio tapes. A woman had donated her collection to the store as a lending library.

My heart beat faster as I held my first Lazaris tape in my hand. I felt like I had struck gold. I felt that I was holding something beautiful and mysterious and sacred in my hand. I stood for a long time, looking through every title. Some were about love, some about confidence, and there was one whole tape on the Higher Self. I paid the nominal rental fee and took a couple home. I wanted to take them all, but the store policy allowed only three at a time.

The first time I heard Lazaris, with that odd accent, their voice was so comfortable and familiar, yet so different. I learned later that not everyone felt comfortable with their voice. Some people did not like it and couldn't relate to the material. I related to the material immediately. I fell in love with it and with Lazaris.

In time, I listened to every tape and watched every video the store carried. I felt like I was receiving these wonderful spiritual truths, that were my own spiritual truths. It felt like a Homecoming. And I met my Higher Self.

In my early days with Lazaris, I ordered the main book, *The Sacred Journey, You and Your Higher Self.*[1] What a fabulous title! I ordered the audio cassette tape of meditations that went with it. I remember that first feeling of proximity to my Higher Self. Sitting with my back against the tree trunk, knowing they were on the other side, reaching my hand around, them reaching out a hand. Our hands touching.[2] That beginning, with a touch: so beautiful!

I ordered another audio cassette tape called the *Gentle Walk: Step-by-Step Intimacy with Your Higher Self*.[3] You can imagine how happy I was—a gentle walk—one I've taken many times over the years.

I learned from Lazaris who my Higher Self was and how they fit into the scheme of things. They said, "Here's the scoop," and guided me right to them. They said, "Here's your Higher Self, Janis. Go, have a relationship (it is limitless) and enjoy. Let them in. Hang out. Do the Dance. Meet and talk and read together and let them show you things and tell you things. Give them as many avenues as you can. Tell *them* things. Tell them about your life and dreams and desires and ask for their help—they love to help.

"Oh, and by the way, they love you and they have been looking forward to being with you. They are very excited that you have found them.[4] Here, let them tell you their name, give you gifts, help you heal and work with you on your spiritual journey. You are not alone. You never have to be alone again."

Thanks to Lazaris, I found my HS in a real and solid way. For me, Lazaris and my HS are inextricably linked. Lazaris changed my life forever. They brought me home to myself and my spirituality. They have walked with me as a friend the whole way, just like they said they would.

Janis Rosen lives in Winnipeg, Canada, and works as a Counselor, Hypnotherapist and Mentor-Coach. You can learn more about her work by visiting www.janisrosen.com. She writes a blog called Stories of Hope and Healing, which can be found on her website. Janis is also an Aromatherapist, who creates beautiful, custom skin creams and perfumes through her company Marilyn Rose. She is a cook, gardener, writer, story lover, and storyteller. Janis is currently writing a book of stories from her life, illustrating the beauty and magic of an imperfect life. When Janis was a little girl, her father would often tell her to get her head out of the clouds. He finally gave up and told her that if she was going to have her head in the clouds, she would also have to learn to keep her feet on the ground. Though she mostly keeps her feet on the ground, she often floats into the ethers to play and bring back wonderful stories.

Endnotes:

[1]Lazaris/Pursel, Jach, "The Sacred Journey: You and Your Higher Self," NPN Publishing, Inc., 1987, Book, e-book.

[2]Lazaris/Pursel, Jach, "The Sacred Journey Meditations," 1987, Concept: Synergy, Audio Recording.

[3]Lazaris/Pursel, Jach, "The Gentle Walk: Step-by-Step Intimacy with Your Higher Self," Concept: Synergy, 1989, Audio Recording.

[4]Lazaris/Pursel, Jach, Accelerated Journey Series, "The Morning Tape, Day 7" (now called, "Morning Blendings, Original Series") Concept: Synergy, Audio Recording.

Is There a Greater Love?

Dietrich von Oppeln

I think it is important to recognize what a tremendous challenge it is for the common person to believe that such a being as Lazaris even exists. Fifty years ago, I would have beaten myself if I had thought of trusting someone like this. I didn't believe in anything. I had dropped out of theology, feeling deeply disappointed, joined the military, came back, tried theology again, and then delved deep into the nihilistic way of looking at life as a meaningless pile of years floating by. I was extremely unhappy, knowing deep down that God existed, but I couldn't find him anywhere. I tried all kinds of therapies. Among them was a Janov therapy (primal scream), which plunged me even deeper into misery and despair. I was making music back then, but it was more like Pink Floyd,

Santana, and the like, often dark and full of melancholy. I tried to break free with drugs, but they got me nowhere but deeper into my own abyss.

The change took place in Munich in 1976, when I attended a seminar led by Rannette Nicholas. She showed us another way to approach life. For me, it was the beginning of a new hope that life has more to offer than just survival. There was a lot about purpose, value, communication, and the sacredness of being. I attended her seminars and annual programs for years.

Around 1988, Rannette discovered Lazaris. She was enthusiastic about Lazaris' music and teaching. She freely and generously shared it with those taking her courses. In one of her seminars, she showed us a video recording that began with this sentence in the opening credits: "There are other ways to grow than through pain and suffering." This touched me deeply. In the years that followed, Rannette even gave up her own work and connected many people with Lazaris. At that time, I also started my own seminar business. I, too, brought many with me to legendary places, such as the Golden Gate Hotel and the Sofitel in San Francisco, the Crowne Plaza in Los Angeles, and the Renaissance Hotel.

I admire and love Jach for channeling Lazaris for so many years for so many. Jach did this in a full trance, and most of the credit went to Lazaris. He ran a business like this while simultaneously dealing with so many different realities, so many different needs and sensitivities. It's something to keep a business successful and reliable that is absolutely not part of the mainstream and has certainly been a target of attacks from time to time. Despite the support of those who so lovingly assisted at each event, how much envy and jealousy were there, too, at times? Envy, jealousy, and rage are truly loaded subjects. I worked with the tape about these emotions for a whole year. They are some of the most important issues, not only for me, but for the entire world.

This is what I found so good about Lazaris: he dealt with topics that are certainly not popular. Pain, Shame, Shadows, Nemesis, Wounding, Dark Wood, Crisis, and Depression...to name a few. I don't know of any other channeled entity that has worked with people in this unique way. And so profound. He opened our eyes to where we need to be healed in order to receive a new world, a world we all long for.

Lazaris also opened unknown portals for me and us: Sirius, Lemuria, the Between, the Imaginal Realm, Magic, and Mystery. And a future which we can create. Really? The future, not the past, creates the present? And, even more, access to our Higher Self, a part of me that I didn't know existed at all! I discovered a whole new understanding of the Soul and unseen friends. As a theologian who had a male god only, learning about the Goddess as creator was transformative for me.

And there is a home! A home that awaits us! So, we are not lost, we are found! And the Underworld is not hell; there is none. It is, in fact, a wonderful magical realm with so many opportunities and places. "And all is right in the Underworld." How I loved, and love, that sentence!!

And then there are those wonderful, guided meditations. I've done at least one a day for over twenty years now. Always in the afternoon. This certainly contributed to the good health that I have today at the age of 75 (2020). And the amazing *Crisis Tape*[1]...how often it has it saved me in times of despair.

Also, the Nature Spirits and Faeries. The Faeries are mighty entities, so different from the depiction in fairy tales. It is pure grace to have one of them as a friend, because they were so disappointed in mankind. Awesome are the Archetypes and the Valley of Giants, the Magic Mill, the Double Tetrahedron and Cosmic Dances that are sometimes even scary in meditations in their majestic grandeur. There are worlds out there...dive in, Magicians!

I trusted Lazaris because of the abundance of subjects, his continuity, and the empathetic way he approaches human life. To hear that there are only a handful of adults in the world shocked me and made me curious. So, what is an adult? An adult is a responsible person, who knows that he or she is creating their own reality.

What? For real? How about God's plan? How about fate and karma? How about the randomness of what happens in life? At the same time, I felt the awful truth. Shattering, shocking and liberating: I am not an adult. And I create my own reality even when I deny it. So, I'm sitting at the red button that could smash or save the world. My world. My reality. It became mine. And, with that, began numerous questions. Why do I feel the way I feel? Why am I so blocked in certain areas of my life? And the answer came: there is shame and pain. There is a negative ego that wants to destroy me. For years, it was about healing, changing beliefs, new awareness, and recreating myself. Often painful, often desperate, sometimes deep in the dark. And then joy, hope, even bliss, magic and miracles when I came out.

One of the greatest gifts from Lazaris for me was Lemuria. Even as a child, I dreamed of a world where everything was fine. I saw it as an island, golden, colorful, full of music and light. People loved each other, animals were our brothers and sisters, and nature was full of Magic. In my first intensive in 1989 entitled *Your Private Magic*,[2] Lazaris took us to Lemuria in a meditation that was so alive for me in its images, sounds and smells that I felt like I was actually there. Lazaris even took us to a Crystal City, where I met sages and immersed myself in bliss and spirit among buildings made of music. Lazaris led us to meet a friend there, who would give us a gift, which would be an indication of our destiny. A translucent being came up to me with such a smile and handed me a crystal that said: "You will bring Lemuria into the world." Seven years later, I wrote my first book, *Lemuria, The Land of Golden Light*,[3] and, two years later, *The Crystal Cities of Lemuria*.[4] I dedicated both to Lazaris.

People then asked me if I could do seminars on Lemuria, so I started my seminar business, www.lemuria.de. My seminars are all about what I am working on in myself.

Since 1989, I have gone to at least one, but usually two or three, Lazaris events every year, often with friends, and later with clients. Something strange always happened when I walked into the room and Lazaris came through Jach. It was like no time had passed between the last event and this current one. Every time, I cried because I was home again. Being in this room was all that mattered. Surely, all of you who write here have a similarly deep personal relationship with Lazaris. The happiness when I received my crystal during the Crystal Ceremony…I felt Lazaris was so close, and the feeling was indescribable. Every time, it was like a moment in eternity…just Lazaris and me. As if I was the only one standing there at that moment. I felt Total Love—and seen. And the precious Magic

Times! What a deep experience for those who were "the lucky ones" and for all those in the room. And the blendings…and…and…

Around 2006, I began thinking about the music in Lazaris' meditations. I got how important music is to Lazaris. I realized that he used the resonances of the music to increase the impact of what he said in the meditations. Since I had been making music for the guided meditations in my own seminars for a long time, I had the idea to record some pieces for Lazaris. I sent them to Jach as a gift of gratitude for all I had learned and received and was able to give to others.

So, I sent the first six pieces to Jach in 2007. For months, I listened to the new meditations, but my music did not play. I then sent another eight pieces, but, still, they weren't used in the meditations. I thought, *Well, they were probably not good enough.* Then Lazaris used a title at the 2008 event in Maui. It was called "Celebration".[5] Later, he used two more pieces.

Of course, I was happy about it, but there was also a strange conflicting feeling, a feeling of shame and doubt. *The music is not good enough, not good enough for Lazaris* was rattling around in my mind. I was constantly criticizing myself and was barely able to follow the meditation. This inner battle went on for a few years. However, it didn't stop me from sending new pieces over and over again. When I learned the name of a year, I created titles for the resonance of that year. Sometimes even directly for the topic of an event. Since I did all pieces in my small studio at home, I experimented with all kinds of sounds and samples. It was also very important for me to find a way to give the Goddess a voice. "Remember the Love…" (CD 3)[6] is one of the titles Lazaris often played when it was about the Love of the Goddess.

Today, I can hear my compositions in the meditations with no problem. Now I can see, and even enjoy how they harmonize with what Lazaris says and does. Not only did Lazaris inspire me to produce enormous amounts of music over the years (now 145 titles), but he also freed and healed me of my most restrictive blockages. The blockage of not being good enough, that of self-importance and perfectionism. With his help and benevolence, it turned into Self-trust, Self-love and Self-confidence. My music is becoming better and better. He helped me to stay loyal to my first love, which always was and is Music.

Is there a greater Love in the Universe?

Dietrich von Oppeln lives in Germany, near Cologne, with his wife, a teenage daughter, three dogs and a cat. Originally he wanted to become a Protestant pastor, worked some years as a high school teacher and then turned to New Age Spirituality being now an author, seminar leader, artist and musician. www.lemuria.de and www.lemuria.online.

As a thank you for purchasing this book, Dietrich offers you access to his "Music for Lazaris" online playlist, over one-hundred forty titles, and invites you to download ten titles of your choosing. Just send him an email via info@lemuria.de, and he will send you the access information. Although this offer doesn't have a firm expiration date, please understand it may end at some point after the initial publishing of this book.

Endnotes:

[1]Lazaris/Pursel, Jach, "The Crisis Tape, Accelerated Journey Series," NPN Publishing, Concept: Synergy, 1992, Audio Recording, Meditation.

[2]Lazaris/Pursel, Jach, "Your Private Magic," Concept: Synergy, 1989, Intensive Workshop. Discussions, Meditations, Magic Time.

[3]von Oppeln, Dietrich, "Lemuria, das Land des goldenen Lichts," Book, Ch.Falk-Publishing, 1997.

[4]von Oppeln, Dietrich, "The Crystal Cities of Lemuria," Book, Ch.Falk-Publishing, 1998.

[5]von Oppeln, Dietrich, "Celebration," Music for Lazaris, CD2, 2007.

[6]von Oppeln, Dietrich, "Remember the Love," Music for Lazaris, CD3, 2010.

Time Passages

Tysa Goodrich

An atmospheric hush rolled in around the jewelry counter, disguised in feminine chatter freewheeling over clearance tables. On the far side where he stood, the air came alive, like how it does before a thunderstorm, deceptively still. I hadn't noticed his presence, at least not by my usual measuring sticks—my five senses—the *real* stuff of my existence, like being inside my body with its all-too-familiar cushiness since the pregnancy. Here on the first floor of Columbus, Ohio's preeminent downtown department store, a glimmer of light was about to arrive at the end of a very long dark tunnel, wherein dwelt the *interminable quagmire (i.q.)* that followed high school graduation and delayed my first day of college by two—and one-quarter—years.

Inauguration of the *i.q.* was the day I ran away from home with my boyfriend.

Where I soon discovered a cold and empty world of no furniture, mustard sandwiches, and a visit to the free clinic. Upon examination, I was informed of the pregnancy. Straightaway I returned home and resumed my role as problem daughter to the man held in high esteem by his congregation. I made a choice without provocation to keep my baby, be married in the church, by my father, and start an adult life— which soon thereafter went into suspension.

They call it preterm labor. My teenage husband—who looked a lot like guitarist Johnny Winter—ran to the corner gas station because we had no phone, called my father to come get me because we had no car. Dad ran stoplights while I lay on the back seat, not silently, hurting. *Get me to the hospital on time.* I gave birth to a one-and-a-half-pound boy and saw my tiny son once, quiet in his incubator. Then he was helicoptered to Children's Hospital. And died the next morning. Easter morning, April 2, 1972. My wounded soul stared back at me through the golden spill of sunrise beyond my hospital window.

The part of me left standing escaped south to Atlanta with my husband, where I got a waitress job at Gigi's Pizza, played *John Barleycorn Must Die* on the turntable incessantly, bought my first VW Bug—fire-engine-red—and not long after, drove it back to Columbus where I'd lost my standing at a prestigious music school, got divorced, and began my higher education at Ohio State.

I didn't know there was a real place called Faerie Realm, or that a portal had opened in my world, in downtown Columbus. I was oblivious, rummaging through the sales basket, untangling scarves. Until a silky fabric the color of burnt orange draped over my arm, and a battalion of goose bumps alighted the tiny hairs. Electricity filled the air. I lifted my gaze to meet his. I had no idea I possessed unfamiliar senses, or that they'd been around since the wee days of childhood—just got lost for a while in the rigors of growing up. I couldn't have known that my future, and the past, were all woven into a single fabric of time—including the interminable quagmire that led to this moment in September of 1973—me, twenty years old, standing at the jewelry counter getting distracted from the pain.

Thirty-five years later, in September of 2008, an atmospheric hush rolled in around a gathering of human and faerie magicians in Maui.[1] A balmy breeze entangled white curtains slid to their open-aired position, revealing a tropical paradise beyond the perimeter. The see-through fabrics billowed in and out of the hotel ballroom, reminding the humans that space was not fixed, and time was not linear. Each meditation took us beyond space-time, through the ether, and into faerie. Did the humans see the faeries sitting among us? Maybe. Were we aware of their presence via our unfamiliar senses? Indubitably so, without certainty or proof.

This was not my first faerie realm workshop facilitated by the channeled being named Lazaris, who brings magnificent love from far beyond human and faerie planes of existence, helping mapmakers heal wounds and work their magic. Over the past twenty years, Lazaris had become my eternal friend. He was the one who guided me through my first entry into faerie realm, when I was deathly afraid—a past lifetime abduction fueling the fear.

By the time I arrived in Hawaii, I had already forged a relationship with my faerie friend and understood that his realm occupied the same earth fabric as the human realm; it existed in the same time but in a much different space. The breadth of magic in the Maui workshop catapulted me through the infidelity of time, and reawakened a memory, long past relegated to the cobwebbed attic of my subconscious. It was he, my faerie friend, the one I came to know in my fifties, who had visited me on that fall September day in 1973, when I was only twenty. He entered through a faerie gateway—which are sometimes hidden in back alleyways of big city asphalt jungles—to check up on me. He stepped from his world—less encumbered by rules and time, a much wilder place, freer, where nature is exalted—into my world of straight lines, measured time, skyscrapers, factories, and department stores.

He stood there, regarding me from the far side of the jewelry counter, his smile subtle and pure, his face seeming to be modeled from earth, his skin as consensual as wildflowers in mud after a rainstorm. His eyes were evanescent veils between worlds, like radiant sapphires suffused with indigo, an evening sky, capable of siphoning out my pain. In my whole life, no one as beautiful had ever crossed my path. He bypassed my flatlined world and opened a door to a different future. The light in his eyes was the light at the end of that long dark tunnel.

The burnt orange scarf floated to the floor. When I stooped to pick it up, it had disappeared. I lifted back to standing, and he was gone. In a foreign desperation, I walked around the rectangular cavern looking for him. Then through the revolving door I stepped outside to the concrete jungle of my human world, yearning for something more, wishing to see him there, but he was not.

My faerie friend had chosen an interesting time and place for this brief encounter, one that would whisper to my future and drop a hint as I looked back—that perhaps he already knew me. The name of Columbus's downtown shopping icon was Lazarus Department Store.

In time, the younger me would forget. In the years that followed, snippets would wake up inside, especially during the time I toured as a rock keyboardist and vocalist. The yearning never stopped. I spent six solid years on the road, working in bands, travelling through twenty-six states and Canada. From the outside looking in, I was living my dream. From the inside looking out, there was a chasm of separation. But I kept going. I found solace in the music, and in the quietude of hotel rooms, devouring every book I could find on dreaming and metaphysics. I started meditating. By the early eighties, I was incorporating mystical themes into my songwriting. I once wrote a song entitled "Somewhere Beyond the Storm"—*a place beyond my shame.*

I moved to Los Angeles, a dream I'd had since wee childhood. The first book I read in California was Shirley MacLaine's *Out on a Limb,*[2] which introduced me to channeling and the concept of channeled beings. I was spellbound. I began inching closer to that something I still couldn't imagine. While I journeyed, I met and married the drummer of my first L.A. band, and gave birth to my daughter Terra, whose determined soul informed me of her name even before I became pregnant. When she was almost two and I in the middle of another divorce, a Malibu psychic guided me to Lazaris.

Twenty years later, I'm sitting in that Maui workshop. And in the middle of a *magic time*—during someone else's talk with Lazaris—I connected the disassembled dots in a rush of revelation. My faerie friend had visited the post-wounded interminable-quagmired me, at a time when I couldn't have fathomed a portal opening between realms.

But I *realized* it for her, for that me thirty-five years younger. Love can do that.

During our lunch break, some friends and I drove to the Iao Needle, a natural rock formation standing twelve hundred feet above the floor of a sacred lush valley. The terrain was evocative of the meditation I'd just had with my faerie friend in his realm. I have a long tradition of mailing picture postcards to my daughter from the places I visit—did the same with my parents when I was touring as a musician during my twenties. In the Iao Valley gift shop, I chose a festive *Aloha from Maui* postcard for Terra. I also purchased one for myself, with the image of the verdant Iao Needle—to remember. Because in this place I still sensed him with me. I slipped both postcards into my canvas tote and carried them back to the hotel. As I often do, I came into the workshop room early, sat in the stillness. I reached into my bag to write my daughter's postcard, and discovered not two, but three. A duplicate of the Iao Needle had somehow made its way into my bag. As I pulled out the postcards—one *Aloha*, and two *Iao Needles*—electricity filled the air. Just as it had before, when a burnt orange scarf draped over my arm, and a battalion of goose bumps alighted the tiny hairs.

I came to find you. I may have come to remember you, I'm not sure.

Tysa has been a professional musician, composer, and songwriter for five decades. She studied music theory and composition at Ohio State, then went out on the road as a rock keyboardist and vocalist in 1977. She has written stories about the crazy shenanigans of touring musicians—playing East Coast mafia clubs, a band equipment hijacking, meditating at the Holiday Inn in Atlanta, and late-night UFO encounters while motoring between gigs. In 1983 she drove herself and her dreams across the country to Los Angeles, and since has composed songs and soundtracks for film and internet, produced two meditation music CDs, and sang "Star Spangled Banner" at Dodger Stadium. She wrote two full-length screenplays and received an honorable mention for a 101-word flash fiction. Her six-word life story was published in a NY Times bestseller anthology of six-word memoirs. She is an intuitive counselor and medium, and writes a Creativity and Chaos blog as coyotescribe, which includes posts about healing, metaphysics, and working magic. She is currently completing a twentieth-century historical fantasy novel.

Endnotes:

[1]Lazaris/Pursel, Jach, "A Bountiful Feast of Magic: A Union of Human and Faerie Magicians" ~ September 2008, The Year of Freedom," Concept: Synergy, 2008, Audio Recording, Evening Lecture, Meditation.

[2]MacLaine, Shirley, "Out on a Limb," Bantam Books, 1983, Book.

Suggested titles:

Lazaris/Pursel, Jach, "Mystical Other: Beyond the Conscious Mind ~ December 1997, The Year of Empowerment," Concept: Synergy, 1998, Audio Recording, Evening Lecture, Meditation.

Lazaris/Pursel, Jach, "Healing the Adolescent Within," Concept: Synergy, Connecting with Lazaris series, Discussion, Meditation.

Love is Like a Set of Matriochkas

Carole Sainte-Marie

Life unfurls itself like a long ribbon that clumsy young hands try to manipulate. Inevitably, twists, rumples, and knots are formed, needing corrective adjustments to reinstate its linear perfection. After many trials and errors, a splendid bow might finally adorn the gift wrapping, more knowledge and *savoir faire* having been acquired in the process.

Such is each human path, shaped by the interaction of experiences gained through failures and successes. Viewed from a higher perspective, our lives would all be worthy of becoming a theater drama of incomparable beauty, accompanied by the understanding of how entanglements are formed and dissolved. However, the main thread, the underlying cause uniting together all scenes, all situations, is Love in its different aspects.

I am personally fortunate and most grateful that, in the late '70s, when I felt I should cut my stained and entangled ribbon, Lazaris appeared in my life and helped me straighten it. Videos speaking about Dominion and Manifestation acted like the ray of a lighthouse over a troubled sea. I realized I was offered the possibility to see the ribbon deposited in my hands stretch long enough to allow the formation of a proper bow before I could proclaim that my job is done.

So, within the many discoveries and reawakening of knowledge sleeping in the recesses of my soul, I could, as well, get reacquainted with Love, that feeling encompassing many forms and reaching different levels. It explains why, in my mind, Love can easily compare to a set of *matriochkas*, those lovely painted Russian dolls all fitting into a larger one. As each is unique, so is every loving experience. Under Lazaris' guidance, I saw the dolls I already possessed shine more brilliantly. More importantly, I was offered the opportunity to augment my collection of dolls, allowing me to find the mother *matriochka*, the one in which all others can be inserted.

Looking back at the knots and marks appearing on my extended ribbon of life, I can pinpoint when, where, and how changes occurred within me, embellishing each of my precious dolls. As I narrate what happened, maybe you will have a more appreciative look at the ones you own.

I seem to have been born wearing the armor of the knight, ready for the next battle as soon as vanquished in the last defeat. Thinking about it, aiming at becoming a Warrior of the Light and later, Keeper of the Flame, was probably always present in my soul in the form of a seed ready to sprout in the open air. On the physical plane, I avoid dark and cold places, for my need for light and warmth is as essential as food and sleep. And what is Love if not an expression of Light and Warmth? It did not guarantee easy relationships though. Many a regretful choice led me to loosen my shield as I lowered the drawbridge and opened the gates of my fortress, my heart, only to see it sacked, left in ruins. I then concluded that relationships are complex puzzles and somehow, I always seem to be missing a piece. But, since the need to love is embedded within our genes, this left me with the role of caring for people I never met and never will, defending less fortunate souls. Faraway starving communities occupy the top of the list.

For a long time, I felt like an alien who never perfectly fit in the world, as if ignorant of the codes that everyone seemed to possess. It was not easy to be different without knowing why, as, physically, I met the norms. Were my actions clumsy, the acuteness of my emotions seen as a weakness? Or maybe my readiness to fight for what I esteemed as being fair and just did not please everyone. Who knows what we project onto others? Without much surprise, two mediums told me that I came from a place called Elsewhere. Having some knowledge about our stellar origins, I let the idea sink in, somewhat feeling delighted about it. Later, Sirius and the Pleiades became predominant names stirring and exciting some molecules within my body, nurturing a sense of belonging. At last, I could spot a star or two as a possible Home…

As I walk on this planet, though, I am touched by Nature and its wonders. They make my old pump beat at a different and soothing tempo. I have even known ecstasy looking at a beautiful panorama, especially if it had the aspect of the first morning on Earth. Music and art can produce a similar effect because, to me, Beauty is the sister of Love. Can I confess that I fell for some trees, magnificent ones, whose death, when it occurred, broke my heart? I marvel at the sight of a simple flower. After all, each one, as it was once said, is dressed more preciously and elegantly than King Solomon, whom I revere greatly, ever was.

A beautiful *matriochka*, wearing the most lustrous coat, represents the animal kingdom. So many have crossed my path, barking, meowing, tweeting. All so unique that none of them will ever be forgotten. Alive, or in the form of a souvenir, their innocence and authenticity often bring tears to my eyes. I am deeply touched by the majesty of the wild ones and the trust of the domesticated others. I dream of this Eden where our souls, returned to a primal purity and radiance, would allow us to walk, fearless, among the most ferocious.

Thinking that a person can love solely what can be seen and touched, my set of painted dolls included my entourage, my job, some hobbies, and a few material things, whereas many people would add their adoration for the God of their faith before considering the list complete. Questioning religion at an early age, I was not interested in attending services in buildings erected on popular highways. They offered no answer to that unnamed something I was looking for, no guidance in my personal quest. I found it more interesting to venture on roads less traveled, looking for more fluid and secretive sacred sites. However, being attracted by the bright light that shined so far away, on a seemingly unreachable horizon, I came to realize that even Stonehenge was still too physical to meet my expectations, for I had found the terrain does not only stretch horizontally, but vertically as well. The temple, such a traveler comes to realize, is well hidden, nestled within the body itself, a hub through which receiving and dispensing converge.

Lazaris appeared in my life on what I would call a moonless and starless night, filled with despair and desolation. A tiny spark of hope, an inaudible invitation to enter a bookstore, and I found myself desiring to explore this new venue that seemed to correspond even better to my spiritual journey. As soon as this multi-dimensional entity entered the scene, new visions started to appear through a dissipating fog, new hopes emerged, and new dreams were meant to be manifested. Nature somehow became even more of a cathedral, the beach a place to dream, and all I had to do to access them was to close my eyes and imagine. It used to hurt not to be able to share such an extraordinary adventure with a peer. With time, though, it sank within me that loneliness is only an illusion, and solitude is an asset. In truth, I had already explored different paths, had learned about the existence of the Goddess, and wished the fairies were real, but they were all distant entities for whom the thought that I mattered was a far-fetched one.

Dressed in the costume of The Fool, carrying my small backpack of knowledge, fears, love, and pains, I accepted to listen to the voice of Her messenger and new friend so that he/they could guide me to places I had never ventured. Encouraged by Lazaris' love, I faced my challenges and hurts, and healed many. During that process, I have met my Soul and my Higher Self and now feel that they take care of me like any bigger *matriochka* would, enveloping and protecting a smaller one. I finally had found the proper road leading to the discovery of who I AM. I am now returning Home.

Carole Sainte-Marie is a retiree from the travel industry living in Montreal, Quebec. Born with a warrior spirit, she is an activist of animal, environmental, and human rights causes. Her love for crystals led her to study gemology, and she did Tarot consultations on a professional basis. Her hobbies include photography and the study of foreign languages, while her passions are equally shared between animals and writing. She has followed many literary creation courses and still leads a circle of amateur writers. These activities helped bring to fruition two novels in the French language, one of them expected to be published in 2022. She also writes in different genres and had the pleasure of winning the first prize for a short story. Most of her work is influenced by her spirituality, sometimes offering an introduction to the Goddess and different cultures, including the Fairy Realm.

Living the Magic

Patricia Walkar

I've always believed in magic. Indeed, as a child, I did…what child doesn't? But as I grew toward adulthood, my belief in magic went underground, buried by the press of cultural norms. I surrendered to hard work and carefully pleasing others to get my basic needs met and, maybe a dream or two, fulfilled. I came to believe in the physical and respond only to those things that I could smell, touch, taste, see, and hear. Decades later, when I first met Lazaris, I was reawakened to the truth: that I create my reality, that life is a magical soup that I can make, stir, and flavor to delicious ends. What's more, I learned I could stir the brews of other soups, of the world's soups, for the benefit of humanity and of all that is good, true, and beautiful. I could see what was happening in the world, and with magic, with my love and will, change it.

This day in April 2020 a viral pandemic is raging around the world. Medical experts have told us to reduce social contact and stay at home. Many businesses are closed. When we must leave our homes, we wear masks to stop transmitting the virus through our breathing or coughing. Some of us are resisting. Tempers are flaring, violence is threatening. And on this day, a security guard is killed when he asks someone to put on a mask. I must respond.

I am at home. I have been sitting on my couch for such long periods that I have dented the sofa cushions. But this interruption in my usually active life has released me from my self-inflicted duties and obligations. There are no deadlines to meet, no volunteer commitments to fulfill, no visitors nor visiting on my calendar. It feels good to back away from routine. It is good to be in this solitude. And, it's time to intervene, to work magic.

I quiet myself. I choose a deep green calcite sphere, the newest crystal in my collection, to be my companion. It has a rainbow, a plate-like inclusion, that is mysterious and inviting. As I cradle the globe in my palms, I feel its aliveness, its softness, its throbbing creativity. I close my fingers around it and press my desires and visions into its welcoming body. Placed securely on a table in front of me, it will be both witness and participant in this magical working.

I close my eyes and breathe deeply to relax. I notice the hum of the heater. The sound soothes me into the folds of my imagination where, gradually and elegantly, I emerge in my safe and sacred place. Surrounded by trees and flower beds, I stand, pulling at sweet-smelling grass with my bare toes. A special tree rises behind me, its protective limbs connecting to the sky, its rooted skirt adorning the ground. I turn and touch its grooved bark, pushing my fingers into the creases. I reach my arms wide around its trunk as I pull my body tight into its familiar presence. We have known each other for many lifetimes. I center.

A coolish breeze strokes my arm and draws my attention away. I release my tree. Turning, I see splotches of sunlight dropping on the ground and making a path. I follow this path onto a wide meadow that hosts a dance of wind and wildflowers. There, I bend, and with my fingers, I draw a circle on the ground. Short grasses move aside as I press into the moist soil. My nostrils flare at the sweet decay of earth. Beginning slowly and moving carefully, I make the circle about eight feet in diameter, ending where I began. I stand and look down, satisfied with my work. I place the arches of my feet squarely over the line with my toes pointing to the circle's center. Earth's energy ascends into my body. I look up at the sky, blue as lapis. I open the lens of my heart to call my team, as I imagine their warmth, their substance, their light and life, their movement, their voice.

I look around the meadow. A perimeter of trees sways slightly, a bird stops chirping, a dust swirl lifts leaves from last year's fall. A slight breeze tickles my left ear until I look in that direction. There is nothing. And then, a shift of energy as if heat rising radiates in that spot over there. It coalesces…slowly, taking shape, taking form. It moves. It builds. It becomes a solid male form…a Magician's Magician, a Siriun. His face is a carving of kind strength. His robes, weighty with color, pulse dense purple, bluish woody green, deep ruby. A staff leans against his right shoulder. His presence speaks of authority without the crutch of words. In his hands rests a sphere, a globe of milky crystal alive with rainbows that flit and vanish where his gaze touches. He nods a greeting in my direction. I nod in reply. He, assertive but respectful in a masculine way, positions himself on the circle to my left at one-quarter the round.

A tall, willowy female steps gently into the right of my visual field. Her chin, tilted up, pushes her face and heart to the sun. Whiter than white, her gown touches softly to the ground where her feet, bare, communicate with Earth, with the Mother. She is a Sage Healer of Lemuria. Her heritage comes of the Dreamers of the most ancient times. Her long fingers embrace a globe of fluid light, a crystal that seems not to be solid at all. She gazes at me through eyes full of secrets, secrets of the healing that love knows. She nods a greeting and, with feminine grace, she moves to my right on the circle at one-quarter the round.

Pop! Without prelude, a youngish fairie stands in front of me. He is my height, wiry and intense. With his Will barely contained, he presents his globe for review. It is blessed green, the green in the middle color range. It is not dark forest nor spring greenish; it is the green "in the between." His clothes are pieces of brown draped and hinged together invisibly and perhaps by magic alone. He wears a shield of bark on his back; the strap of it crosses his chest, highlighting his slender figure. His black eyes hold mine as he asks, "Yes?"

"Yes," I reply.

He takes his place on the circle across from me at half the round.

I am in my place on this ring of magic. I am resolute, determined to make a difference. I, too, hold a globe, a crystal birthed with so many message plates, rainbows, and mineral embers that I cannot see through it. It is heavy with magic. The globe was a gift from Sirius. Lifetimes ago in Lemuria, I was charged with teaching six youngsters, each of whom had an awesome destiny. They needed guidance to develop their skills, but they were difficult, and I did not know how to reach them. Frustrated, in a maze of confusion, I looked to Sirius for help. Then, in a dream, a globe of light appeared, a crystal companion. Hope filled me in my solitary walks through forests and rocks, and in my rest and meditation along a lake. One day, after a mediation, a sparkling sphere, an Ancient One, a Fire Ball, rose from the lake. It was my crystal companion. I became its keeper, and it became my guide. It fired the creativity of each child, and each found their destiny. Three became Dreamers and one an Elder Dreamer. One became a Sage Healer, and another a Sage Witness. The last became an artist, a painter and a bard, a Sage Teller of Tales, a Wise One.[1]

Conscious of my magical heritage, I take a silent moment. I know the power entrusted here; it humbles me. My team is silent for a moment too.

Now ready, we begin. We survey each other, and then, together as one, we raise our globes. They transform into spheres of light, brilliant, bright. They expand. They grow larger and larger, and larger still. They touch, they meld, they encompass each other. They reach toward the sky, transforming into a cone of energy, a force growing higher and higher to ten, then twenty feet tall and more.

Into this cone, I put my desire to cool the violence. I want more kindness, more thanksgiving, more truth, more beauty. I imagine people smiling, and moving carefully, thoughtfully around and toward each other. I hear words of offered help and thankfulness...just a few words, filtered through their masks. I think of the irony of how a mask covers the lie of an insincere smile, how it reduces the clutter of conversation, how it makes us look into each other's eyes and, for a second, see each other's souls. I project images of beauty...of places on Earth that have left me enchanted...the infinite delicacy of flowers, the iridescent colors of magma frozen above ground, the grand of canyons and mountains...a kaleidoscope of beautiful images. I feed all of this into the cone. I whisper, "This or better with harm to none."

I sense my team putting their images into the cone. I do not know their specifics, nor do I need to. Our goal is the same: to seed the world with kindness, thanksgiving, truth and beauty. I feel the richness. Richer and richer, deeper and deeper, heavier and yet lighter at the same time, the cone expands in all directions.

Our hearts open, and, as with one thought, we lift the cone to the Goddess. We ask that She respond to our visions, or better, with harm to none. We feel Her love filling the cone, adding to ours. We sense that She contributes what we cannot yet imagine. We sense that miracles are about to happen. She stretches and transforms our cone into a blanket of light.

It spreads over continents and oceans, encompassing humanity, encompassing the world. It enfolds, it comforts, it cools the fear and drama. Our new images emerge, clearer and clearer, lighter and freer, as the blanket of light melts into the world.

Quiet, still, complete. We breathe deeply, richly. We hold each other with our eyes. We contemplate what we have done as our energies cool and calm. Our round, our crystals, our meadow with its surround of trees, come gradually into prominence. Slowly but surely, our faces glow with full grins! We laugh, we move, we dance in celebration and gratitude. We have initiated a change; we have spun a new thread for a world becoming new.

Renewed by magic, and by each other's grace, we wish each other farewell. The Siriun lowers his staff to me, and fades to nothing. The Sage Healer transforms to mist, and is gone. My faerie ally bows curtly before vanishing into a tree. And I find myself in my safe place once again, my bare feet tickled by grass, my back against my tree, my Fire Ball crystal still warm in my hands.

In the days since the magic, I see signs in my community requiring masks and people wearing them. I forgot my mask on one occasion, and a cheerful clerk handed me a mask with a "No worries. Here's one you can have." I went out of town, too, to New York City, where everyone on the street wore masks and social distanced but nodded kindly to each other in greeting. There were fewer sirens than are typical in New York. Peace filled the air. As I stood in line at a parking garage to get my car, a woman with a mask looked at me and said, "You really can see a person smile through a mask. I can see it in your eyes."

So mote it be...and so it is.

Patricia Walkar is an artist, poet and sometime storyteller. She holds BA and MA degrees in communication sciences. During her art career of over two decades, Patricia's work has won numerous awards. Her abstract and floral paintings on silk are known for their beauty and healing impact. Motivated by her spiritual journey, Patricia creates poems that expand the meaning in many of her paintings. Her work has been collected by individuals, corporations and hospitals, and Patricia has presented workshops to artist groups and the general public. Currently, she is creating a book of her paintings and poetry. Her paintings can be viewed at www.patriciawalkar.com and on Facebook at Patricia Walkar. Inquiries about pricing or studio visits can be directed to patriciawalkar@aol.com.

Endnote:
[1]Pursel, Jach, "Fire Ball's Heritage," Provenance Document, 2009.

Imagination Reawakened

Rebecca Cutehands

As I begin to share with you how Lazaris and I found each other, I find myself reminiscing about many moments of the past, when certain teachers, teachings, or adventures came into my life when I was least expecting it, not searching for anything, not looking for answers to any questions...just being in the happening of the moment. As I do this now and look back, I feel as if they were waiting for me to arrive, and that makes me excited and humbled to think what else is waiting for me to simply show up.

Like this one day when I went to Serpent Mound in Ohio. I was only nineteen years old and was traveling there that day for a simple outing with some friends to check out this amazing effigy we had heard about. It was only a four-hour trip from where we lived, so we took off on a beautiful Sunday morning, grabbed some road snacks and our crystals and stones we thought we would bless in the waters that ran through the land there at the mounds. Little did I know, that day would initiate me into my family's heritage and bring me to the sacred road that I was to walk while I am here again.

Once we arrived, we made our way down to the waters, blessed our stones and crystals, and even left a few as offerings. We then headed up to the scenic lookout point. When we reached the top, our eyes fell upon the giant serpent that rises out of the earth and stretches itself across the land with the cosmic egg within its mouth; this is a vision I will never forget, it has imprinted on my soul, and I am grateful for that. As we started to make our way out towards the entrance, we heard a native drum being played, and a big group of people were gathering in a circle getting ready for some kind of ceremony, so we headed over to check it out. Within a minute or two, I was picked out of the crowd by the Indigenous man leading the ceremony. As his eyes were traveling through the crowd, I felt inside of myself that he would call upon me for something. Somewhere, I already knew this was going to happen, and he did. He asked me if I could speak the medicine of the North, and, even though my friends and I gathered for ceremony for many years prior to this moment, those were nights we would gather on the full moon, laughing, praying, and exploring our adolescence during rituals that felt innocently powerful. However, this ceremony felt different; this felt like I was being pulled in and up to sit at the adult table. It felt like this was a moment that had been created for me to weave into something bigger than I knew at the time.

When the circle of prayers came to me, my tears were already falling upon the earth. Hoping that my words would sound as elegant as those who spoke before me, I started to speak. I felt like my words were carried from another space and time; hearing them flow from me was truly inspiring. It was as if they were there all this time, and they were waiting for this moment. When I opened my eyes and looked at my friends, they, too, were crying, and I realized at that moment why they call it "medicine." It is medicine, all of it, all of our words, actions, responses, circumstances, challenges, celebrations, all of it; it's medicine that feeds us, heals us, teaches us, guides us. This was a sacred moment in time that brought me to meeting myself differently, and I was excited, humbled, and ready for more.

Which now brings me to another moment that was waiting for me to simply show up. Over the years, one of my dear friends and I would create time for us to retreat and play in a studio we shared, where we offered our healing sessions, classes, and ceremonies. Depending on what would want our attention, we found ourselves always enthralled in many different types of magical moments. We would clean our crystals to rebuild our stone grids, create sacred oil and water potions, journal, talk, laugh, brainstorm, and would always share in some kind of decadent chocolates. I remember when my friend and I were on one of our retreats, and she asked me if I wanted to do a Lazaris blending. As I found myself saying yes, I also found myself thinking, *What's a Lazaris? And what's blending?*

Either way, it sounded fun and magical, and I could tell that my friend was excited that I had said yes. So she began speaking to me about this Lazaris as she lit some candles, turned down the lights, and asked me to find a place where I felt comfortable sitting or lying down as we listened. I knew right then this "blending" was not a beverage of exotic fruits and vegetables we would be drinking, or a bottle of infused essential oils we would be creating. No, this was something that I was not familiar with and was not expecting. As soon as she started the blending and I heard his voice, I was immediately transcended to a different space of being. I noticed I had a gentle smile on my face as I began to relax and feel as though I was being guided by an old friend. A friend that you can be yourself with and allows you to truly feel comfortable enough to let go and give in to the journey. I realized at that moment that Lazaris was gifting this to me, reminding me to trust and to just let go. What a beautiful gift, what a sacred blessing. To be able to truly release the self from the physical body and experience all that is.

So many times during guided meditations, I would hold myself back into my flesh, bound to my body, afraid of experiencing the journey fully, only allowing myself to go so far, afraid to release from the physical world and float or fly into the story. Now I felt bound by nothing, free, free to truly experience. Sometimes I would trust so deeply that I would fall asleep during the blending and wake up and want to listen to it again. Even when I stayed fully present with being guided, I would want to listen to it again. Usually, I would find moments along the way that I missed the first time. Sometimes, even through second and third times, I would hear bits and pieces for the first time. The blessing of trust that I allowed myself to inherit from the blendings catapulted me into a new and exciting relationship with journeying and guided imagery. The feelings and the colors, sounds, and the images, responses, and senses became heightened and uninhibited. I felt truly blessed. My imagination was reawakened. Thank you, thank you, thank you, Lazaris, and thank you to my dear friend who reconnected us.

I revisited many teachings throughout the years, from many different cultures and teachers. I found myself receiving them differently after opening up to such amazing moments of travel with the times I shared in the blendings with Lazaris. Since I was seventeen years old, I have been hosting ceremonies, and I would channel the prayers as we would move around the medicine circle as I still do to this day. The messages come with so much grace, elegance, and power and sometimes move me into tears, but because I was channeling, I didn't get to travel and experience these offerings like the people in the circle. The ones who would attend these ceremonies would tell me how much they appreciated being given a moment that felt so expansive, but so personal, as if the messages coming through were for them alone, and how it allowed them to receive a healing or an opening of some kind.

As I worked with the blendings, I felt the same way. These were moments I was giving myself to let go, to simply receive, travel, heal and experience. Moments where I wasn't the channel or the one leading ceremony, I simply allowed myself to be guided, led, and connected. I truly understood the depth of the connection and the gifts within the channeling that those who sat in circle with me would experience. This has brought me to a place of balance with giving and receiving, with the channeling of messages, and has gifted me a beautiful fulfillment within my life, and I feel truly blessed. Now, when we gather in circle, and I am channeling, I feel my smile is resting on every word that comes through. Knowing that someone is allowing themselves to truly travel and adventure with the messages and the stories being gifted in the moment, just as I do when I'm receiving them from Lazaris.

I have had many people bless me with many gifts in my life. From a smile or a gentle gesture to the healer who came in and assisted me with healing a life-threatening illness. Teachers from different cultures sharing their sacred teachings and trusting me to carry them to the world with authenticity. And yes, Lazaris helping me regain my imagination so that I could manifest and create a world of beauty and love, not just for myself, but for all of Creation. Many beings on my sacred list have made a very beautiful imprint on my soul, and Lazaris is definitely one of them. I am truly, truly grateful.

Rebecca Cutehands lives in Arizona with her husband and two furry friends. She feels absolutely blessed in each day of life, no matter what is brought before her. She is honored to be a student of Creation and is truly grateful for every day she gets to play on this planet. She enjoys guiding and reflecting to her clients healthier and happier ways of being and loves to celebrate ceremonies throughout the year. She offers healing sessions, teachings, workshops and a variety of ceremonies. You can find her at http://www.mountainspiritco-op.com or https://mshec3.com/.

Three Stories from My Journey with Lazaris

Erin E. Kampa

Meeting Lazaris, Meeting Love

It was my 22nd birthday—June 20, 1986—and I was a young adult impatiently seeking the next steps into my real "Life." I was trying on jobs and different college majors. I was frequently frustrated, as nothing seemed to fit. Of course, everyone else seemed to have it together. My good friend Diane had graduated from NYU and was living in the city. For her graduation, I gave her a reading with a psychic we had visited before...of course, I wanted to know more about my future, to "nail it down." And then, the psychic invited us to participate in some psychic development classes on Monday nights. I was intrigued and enthusiastic about exploring more.

The next several weeks were a crash course of everything I had never been exposed to before...chakras, aromatherapy, working with the elements, meditating, crystals...so much, and much of it wonderful. When I look back, it was a preparation for what was to come.

On one of these Monday evenings, our host was going to show us a video of a channeled entity named Lazaris. I went to the class from Connecticut on the train, excited to go to the city on my birthday. I always felt there was magic in the month of my birthday, so I was expecting something extraordinary.

The garden apartment was hot and crowded with about twelve people. We all sat where we fit around a TV. The *Awakening the Love*[1] video began to play. Jach was first explaining how his channeling Lazaris had come to be, who he was, and how Peny was the one that Lazaris came to talk to, and she had graciously decided to share him. It was beautiful in itself. Then Jach followed his preparations and began to go into a trance.

And Lazaris came through. He began to talk about who he was and then outlined the process of Love and what to do, and why to do it. It was amazing to me. My busy brain snapped to attention.

Then, the meditation—so vivid, so focused. I began at a beach and walked into the woods. The trees and earth were vivid and colorful. Following Lazaris' words, we journeyed to a cottage in the woods and met the old man. A friend in a place where we could return. And then we came back...

When I left that evening, I got a cab to Grand Central Station. It was a beautiful breezy night, and the back windows of the cab were open. The warm breeze was whipping around the back seat, and I felt so alive. I wondered if I should doubt—but then I chose, while in my element, Air. I decided that was the most real Love I had ever seen or heard about, and I was going to explore more, learn more about creating my own reality, and find out more about Lazaris. The Love was too Real to leave behind.

Making Love Real

It was 1991 and a warm September night in New York City. I had become a nurse and was meeting friends for drinks with my new boyfriend, Michael. I was a little taken aback at realizing that this could be a "big" love in my life, but I was playing it "loose." We stood in the crowded bar, surrounded by businessmen, and the nurses we came there with, jostled and laughed and enjoyed being young in the city.

Then a girlfriend, Lisa, began to speak to a guy wearing a tie, a businessman coming from work for a happy hour before his train ride home. I'm an outgoing person in the right situation, so I joined in the conversation. Lisa turned to get a drink at the bar for a moment, and I continued talking to the guy about nothing. Then, my boyfriend, Michael, touched my arm and said, "You're here with me." The statement was like a jolt of electricity. I said something like, "Of course, I am." And then I said, "We should leave and go to my apartment." I knew we needed to talk, and not in a loud, smoky bar. I turned to say goodbye to my friends. I was thinking about the vulnerability in his statement. I felt that here was an opportunity to exercise power to make someone else feel insecure, as I had so many times in other relationships.

But then I remembered the love. I remembered the Real Love that I had learned about with Lazaris through many tapes and books since that first night. I reached out to my Higher Self, asking for guidance, as I went home with Michael to discuss this moment of jealousy. Our love was budding, not ready to bloom, and I realized at that moment that I didn't want to trample it with drama or manipulation. I could let go of my history and its influence at this moment.

We returned to my apartment near the hospital. I was opening a bottle of champagne in the kitchen while Michael watched. He stammered a bit, "I'm sorry I was weird in the bar, but it's just that I love you, and I didn't want you to..." His words trailed off. I turned, stricken by the moment, as if I knew this would be the seed of a twenty-year marriage. I hugged and kissed him, I remember. I realized that I needed to be gentle and more vulnerable myself, willing to open myself up to what was Real in the Love before me. I was and will be ever grateful for knowing what Love is. Learning what I learned from Lazaris guided me through a moment that has been one of the most beautiful of my life.

Letting Miracles Be Real

The other striking and life-changing concept that I learned with Lazaris was Creating our own Reality. He offered many techniques we could choose or adapt to our own goals, and I always loved the choice—Lazaris taught us that the ultimate technique is Choice.

My story about choice is also about a miracle—allowing, claiming, and demanding a miracle. One time in my life that this was important and demonstrated strongly, was when I was trying to get pregnant in 2003. I learned with Lazaris that focusing our desire, imagination, and expectations—clarifying our intent—was crucial to creating what we want to create. I had a lot of support, Seen and Unseen, helping me make this dream come true.

I had seen a few doctors over the years to find out why I wasn't able to get pregnant after several years of marriage. My heart knew that it was my destiny to be a mother. So, I found one of the best doctors in Brooklyn.

I forged ahead. I tried medications that didn't work, had tests that were not conclusive. The doctor even told me that both fallopian tubes were probably blocked. She recommended surgery, an option I wanted to avoid. But I demanded that we try a next-level medication—just one cycle. I moved forward with laser-like focus through the procedure and the manifestation.

A few weeks later, I was going home from work on the subway, and I had the moment. I knew the medication could have worked. I felt it deeply in my heart. I closed my eyes and centered, right there on the R train. I reached out to Lazaris, my Higher Self, my Soul, and to God/Goddess/All That Is. I stated, "I want this to be real, to be true. I am ready for this dream to come true." I'm not sure if it was that day, or another soon afterward, when I did a pregnancy test, and it was positive (finally positive). After being told that my tubes were blocked, the meds might not work—all kinds of things that could discourage me—it was the choice, the focus, and the claiming that birthed my miracle, my son, Michael (now a teenager).

Erin E. Kampa lives amongst the trees and hills of northwestern Connecticut. She lives with her husband and teenage son, as well as two awesome dogs. She is incredibly grateful for the Joy in the journey of spirituality and metaphysics as well as the amazing Love of God/Goddess/All That Is.

Endnotes:

[1]Lazaris/Pursel, Jach, "Awakening the Love," Concept: Synergy, 1985, Video (available on YouTube), Audio recording, Discussion, Meditation.

Suggested titles:

Lazaris/Pursel, Jach, "Creating, Building & Keeping Intimate Relationships," 1991, Concept: Synergy, Audio Recording, Discussion, Meditation.

Lazaris/Pursel, Jach, "Becoming a Winner at Living Life," Concept: Synergy, Audio Recording, Discussion, Meditation.

From Restricting Beliefs to Freedom

Dana Cummins

Although my father wasn't still active-duty military when I was born, he raised us as if we were in boot camp, a Catholic boot camp at that. Like most religions, Catholicism shares the great benefits of kindness and love and teachings of hatred and separation. Growing up surrounded by both love and hate in my home life, it took me ages to figure out that I had a choice to keep or trade-up my beliefs.

By age three, I was aware of spirits and beings unseen to most humans. Asking about the ghosts and beings, asking why people wouldn't talk about them, and wondering why people say one thing, but think and felt a way opposite to what they said, were all things that baffled me. I felt the world as too violent, too hypocritical, and filled with too many lies. I spent most of my days hiding and playing under the kitchen table, hoping to avoid the torment of my brothers or father.

My dad told me repeatedly not to play with the outlet under the table, as it would "kill me." Having had enough of living in fear, even at three years old, I wanted out, so I chewed the rubber knob off the bobby pin and stuck it in the socket, hoping to escape from this place. Though I don't remember the moment my fingers exploded from the current, like hotdogs left too long in the microwave, I do remember being so scared of my father for having disobeyed. Although I believed and feared that my father would punish me for that incident, he didn't. My Higher Self took the opportunity to bond with me more, to help me stay here longer. My bond with spirits grew, and I often found them better company than the living. They were my constant companions and playmates throughout my childhood.

My husband and I traveled for seven years in my twenties and landed in Phoenix, Arizona, in the late '80s. Soon after, a new understanding shattered my belief system. I called to tell my father I was getting a divorce. I believed he would disown me the minute I spoke those words. To my astonishment and disbelief, he stood by me and asked me what I needed. I was blown away by his support. I felt confused and torn from a still-raw memory from when I was sixteen.

My mind pulled up the all-too-familiar memory of my parents taking me to live with my rich aunt and uncle up north. After months of rehab from drug addiction and trying to kill myself, I had just left the hospital. I had been jonesing for days leading up to the attempt, as my shipment of speed was four days late. It was a simple choice: I figured I'd rather be responsible for taking my own life than lose it to my father when he found out I was on drugs, or about anything else regarding the life I kept hidden from their world. The words I remember him saying to me on that drive were still vivid: "If you *ever* hurt your mother like that again, I will disown you from this family, and you'll never see any of us again." His threats landed like blows, and I allowed them to direct the course of my life.

That earnest attempt, in which I died but came back to life, led to the conversation in the car with my father in my sixteenth year. In turn, the discussion frightened me, years later, into staying married for eight years to a man who preferred drugs and other women. Shortly after landing in Phoenix, my husband was back on cocaine. After a meltdown, I found the courage to leave him. At the time, it was the second most challenging thing I had ever done. The wound was excruciating and took years to heal.

The fact that I could see a person's spirit was of little help when they rarely choose to live up to the potential that I could see. Unable to differentiate the many voices I was hearing, what I would often listen to was not my Higher Self.

I found the Lazaris VHS series in a local metaphysical bookstore a few months before my divorce. I also found my first mentor, who I moved into my home at the time of my divorce. She would not tell me to leave him but did slide into the role of manipulating me with ease. Allowing new manipulation was another big push in my life. I've had several, as I had often refused the opportunity to live my life owning, claiming, and being in my power. The abuse continued and changed in ways that helped wake me up and change the course of my life. I discovered so much. I learned to quiet the many voices in my head and recognize those who held my highest good in mind. The challenges pushed me to own my power, creating and allowing more love and joy in my life.

Lazaris offered a new understanding of life so profound, I was beside myself. Someone was finally speaking in a way that made sense to me, where I could feel the truth of it, as far as I wanted to go with it. Compassion and love nearly overwhelmed me. Meeting Lazaris was like nothing I could have ever fathomed. My Catholic, military, Adventist background taught me rules, sacrifice, martyrdom, obedience, punishment, unworthiness, not good enough, hate, kindness, and love. The first word I remember out of Lazaris' mouth was love: I'm enough, I'm worthy, I'm loved, I don't need him or anyone, I'm in perfect time, I'm good enough just as I am, I can choose to walk a bit with Lazaris or not, what I desire is perfect! I can experience as much or as little of it as I see fit. My choice is good enough; it is perfect. Lazaris believes in me, even if I don't. And I could *feel* it in *every cell of my being*, that he was telling me the truth. The depth of Lazaris' love equaled only the love I felt meeting Jesus in person at eight years old. No, Lazaris is not Jesus, or at least how I saw Jesus when I was eight. But Lazaris did carry this profound compassion that I sought ever since that meeting. Goodness, Truth, and Beauty oozed from between his words. I felt wrapped and nurtured in love so completely. Lazaris' love had touched me in so many lives; I could feel the recognition and longing from them bleeding through.

By the time I found Lazaris, I had many beliefs and attitudes that were not healthy. None would help me stand in my power except to make money for the family, which was deeply instilled by my hard-working parents.

One of the many early things I heard Lazaris say was that it doesn't matter if you've been working metaphysics for two or twenty years; you can "Allow" great magic to happen in your life just by your "Willingness to Receive." I was so excited by these words that they became my focus for years: willingness, a key in transforming your life into one of grace and ease, beauty and creativity.

After my divorce, I moved to a new city so my ex-husband wouldn't find me. My ex was too hard for me to resist. I loved him very much. I found him sexy, smart, humorous, and well-read. If only he wasn't toxic. The move was to be a big, new start for myself. I found a job and temporary housing while I worked with the Lazaris technique for manifesting. It was after seventeen times of doing the work of the "Meat Grinder"—the process offered in the *Secrets of Manifesting What You Want* tape [1,2]—that I allowed the miracle of a house for free in downtown Prescott. Lazaris created this processing technique for us to find the weak spots, the parts of ourselves that are working against what we say we wish to create and allow. I was all in, determined to create and allow as the magicians who worked with Lazaris for over twenty years. I felt my feelings. I blended. I meditated. I changed my beliefs. I forgave. I sought understanding for many thoughts, feelings, attitudes, and beliefs. The work presented new choices, new attitudes, new thoughts and feelings, and changed my beliefs and decisions. Though it took great effort, and I had to demand it to change, with more determination and will than I have ever displayed in my life prior, it worked. I allowed the house that I had chosen to become mine for a time, for free.

It was a time of great work, astounding magic, and miracles. I continued to submerge myself in the Lazaris material and delved into creating my relationship with him. He helped me expand, explore, and forgive myself for nearly thirty years of repressive beliefs designed to harm me and separate me from my truth. With great compassion and forgiveness, I moved into more of myself, co-creating a whole new life of passion and expression. Still, I had many more lessons to learn regarding owning my power and stopping oppression from surrounding me. The use of humility, willingness, and resonance magic that was inherent within me continued to help me learn and become more. I found happiness, and, for the first time in my life, I wanted to live.

Fifteen years into my work with Lazaris, while heading up a staircase to teach a class and share my love for his material, I looked into a mirror. I saw a dream: a dream of magicians coming together, healing themselves, and helping to heal the world. Then I heard, "It's time to start the Co-Op." What could be better than to create a safe haven for people who are looking for safety and belonging so they could explore, discover, and heal the tormenting aspects of their own lives, as well as help others along their paths? And that is where the idea of Mountain Spirit Co-Op was born. I had been sharing the teachings of Lazaris with students and friends for years. Like a person finding their grace, so eager to share. As sharing was indeed a way for me to learn at a deep, impactful level, I was grateful for the permission. Everyone in the class jumped on board with co-creating the Co-Op, and we opened our doors in three weeks. We are still together today, fifteen years later, always expanding to work with people all over the globe. I am so grateful for the many opportunities Lazaris, Higher Self, Soul, Spirit, Guides, God/Goddess/All That Is have given me.

No one is here to save the world. We're here to share our light, be our light and be in the light of others. In owning and sharing our lights, we will transform the world—starting with ourselves and our loved ones. By making amends for all, we've done as well as all we have allowed. For all we can perceive is all we have done and played a part. Forgiveness must start with ourselves, as change follows forgiveness. If your life is a living hell, please forgive yourself and the whys of those who have hurt you. The change follows forgiveness. Want change? As Lazaris says, "Recognize, Acknowledge, Forgive and Change." For me, choosing daily to live in gratitude has helped me release, heal and forgive the many layers of pain in a graceful and loving way. Wishing you luck in finding what works for you.

Born clairvoyant into a Catholic military family in the Midwest, Dana Cummins used her gifts to escape her reality from an early age. She married young and traveled the country for eight years before divorcing and settling down in Arizona. After healing herself from terminal cancer in 2005, she and a group of friends opened the Mountain Spirit Co-Op to create a safe space of belonging. A place to explore and honor their unique gifts and talents while expanding their spirituality and healing their wounds from the world. She spearheaded the non-profit MsHec3, Mountain Spirit Healing and Educational Center, which opened in 2017, to offer scholarships to those seeking healing yet unable to afford their services. The 501(c)(3) has assisted hundreds with receiving the help they've needed on their healing journeys. Dana enjoys working with practitioners and clients worldwide and looks at the Co-Op as a phone book for people doing good work in their community and the world. She resides in the country outside of Prescott, AZ, with her fiancée, three dogs, and a cat.

Endnotes:

[1]Lazaris/Pursel, Jach, "Secrets of Manifesting What You Want Part 1," January 1985, Video, Audio, Evening Discussion with Meditation.

[2] Lazaris/Pursel, Jach, "Secrets of Manifesting What You Want Part 2," January 1985, Video, Audio, Evening Discussion with Meditation.

First Encounters

Janis Rosen

Maui, September 2008

Over and over again at the Lazaris seminar[1] in Maui, I've been drawn to the ocean, and the final Friday of my second week here is no exception. I take advantage of our two-hour lunch break and head down the beach, to a secluded spot I've discovered, framed by a long piece of driftwood, in a sheltered place near the water.

I close my eyes and lean against the wood, absorbing the heat and enjoying the warm ocean breezes. I listen to the sound of the water lapping against the shore and contemplate my great good fortune at being here—a dream come true. I reflect on my time here, which is almost over.

This is my first trip to Hawaii and my first Lazaris Special Event. When I learn about the seminar, it doesn't matter to me what the subject matter is. That it's in Maui, and with Lazaris, is all I need to decide to come!

I feel elated as I step off the plane into the open air after my long seventeen-hour plane ride from Canada. The warm air embraces me in a nurturing welcome. I am instantly in love with the Maui air. It's like nothing I've felt before, but something I know deep in my Soul. Dressed in my Winnipeg travelling clothes, I want to strip here and now, so I can feel the air against more of my skin.

Standing outside, waiting with my luggage for the shuttle to transport me to the Maui Prince Hotel, little do I know that this trip and this place will have a deep and abiding effect that profoundly changes me forever. It will be a time of first encounters and also a time of remembering.

After checking into my room, I unpack, change and go exploring. The grounds are beautiful and lush, filled with gardens, paths, rocks, pools and little waterfalls. All my senses come alive. This first evening, one of many, I follow the paths leading to the ocean and an open vista stretches before me. I watch the sunset over the ocean, painting the sky orange and golden. The night air is fragrant, soft and sensual. The temperature of the air is so perfect, it's hard to tell the difference between it and my skin. Lazaris calls Maui the Mother Island, and I feel her nurturing presence in all the elements.

I settle into my surroundings, finding an easy flow with the seminar days. There's an enchanted path that leads me to the seminar each morning, and stepping into the seminar room feels like walking through a portal into a magical place. The room is open to the outside, and we can feel the Maui breezes come through. A sense of beauty and celebration accompanies me throughout my stay. I feel excited and at peace at the same time.

We are here to connect with Lemuria the first week and Faerie the second week. What could be better! This is my first encounter with Lemuria. Every night I rest, filled and fulfilled by what Lazaris, Master Weaver of tales and story, myth and legend, then and now, has given and guided us to experience. Lazaris makes Lemuria come alive!

Lemuria, my Lemuria, my home. A land that emerged from the mist when the Vortex of Sirius opened full and wide over 100,000 years ago. Goddess created this land of Lemuria, a land that didn't exist before. She responded to the prayers of the Siriuns to heal the wrongs that were being done on Planet Earth. It is a land where a new kind of human being is created, made from earth and stars, infused with free will. Long ago in Sirius, I heard the call to come to Lemuria, and, here again in 2008, I hear the call once again. It's my past, present and future all connecting and converging.

I am here to reclaim what I lost and forgot when Lemuria was done and slipped back into the mist. To find more of myself, my story, my truth and goodness. Lazaris tells me that Lemuria is a profoundly important part of my framework, and I feel my first connection. Here in Maui, the Mother Island, Lemuria is once again awakened in me, in the fabric of my being, in my Soul and Spirit. It couldn't be more right!

The seminar takes place over the fall equinox, and September 22nd is a free day for us. I decide to spend the afternoon by the ocean, in a personal day of solitude. I open myself to magic and mystery with my activated, seen and unseen senses and the elements exalted. The sun is hot, the air is soft, the water is warm and playful, and Earth offers me her gifts. As I walk to the ocean, beautiful flowers and pods drop at my feet.

I normally prefer to be by the water or on it, not in it, but this day, I spend hours in the ocean, surrendering my body to its movement and playing with the nature spirits. My Spirit lifts. My Soul is at peace. I feel a lightness of spirit and a nurturing that goes deep into my being. I feel joy, celebration and a sense of ecstasy.

My magical child plays. She loves the paths and gardens, waterfalls and pools. Lemuria is an oasis, a place of renewal and a bridge to the future. This time in Maui is an interlude, a reprieve and respite from the life I normally live. Lemuria is a state of mind. My Lemuria, my love, my passion, my beauty.

The first week passes, and we move into the second seminar, with Faerie. This geography is all new to me. Lazaris weaves a beautiful feast of magic and union with Faerie magicians. As we begin, they tell us the seminar room is full of Faerie magicians, and there are many portals here on the Island. I enter this new realm to experience and learn about Faerie. I come to understand that there is a power and substance to their world and to their beingness. They are real to me in new way and not just a figment of my imagination.

On this last Friday of Faerie week, here at my spot by the ocean, I realize that lunch break will soon be over and it's getting time to make my way back to the seminar for our afternoon segment. When I open my eyes, I see a young man, perhaps sixteen or seventeen years of age, walking along the sand towards me. He's too far away yet to make out his features, but I see he is tall, with long legs and a lanky, rhythmic walk.

As he gets closer, I make out more details. He wears a light tee shirt and loose, long bathing trunks. He walks in a measured way on long, narrow, bare feet, water shoes casually slung over his shoulder. I make out his face now, studying it as I try not to stare. He's got a long nose and big eyes, scruffy boy hair.

There is no one else around and, as we encounter each other, we're each aware and politely taking short glances at one other. As he approaches, getting closer, he is smiling to himself. He's looking down, but when he raises his eyes and passes by me, the smile goes to me too. He says hello and nods his big head, and I smile back and say hello.

There's a moment when I wonder if he'll stop and converse, but it passes, and he keeps going around the bend and out of sight. So much is transmitted in that hello. I know he's Faerie. He knows I know. I know it's his first time through the portal and first encounter with a human: me. As he is my first encounter, I am his. He's come through the portal on an adventure, and he's happy.

As I make my way back to the seminar room, I tuck this sweet encounter away in a treasure chest in my heart. Sometimes I think about him and wonder what other wonderful adventures he's been on.

Learn more about Janis Rosen on page 4.

Endnotes:

[1]Lazaris/Pursel, Jach, "Lemuria Revisited: Illuminating Lemurian Nights, Congress of Magicians, and Calling the Lemurian Dreamers and Sages, A Gathering of Magicians" and "A Bountiful Feast of Magic: A Union of Human and Faerie Magicians" September, 2008, Workshops in Maui, Hawaii.

Suggested Titles:

Lazaris/Pursel, Jach, "A Bountiful Feast of Magic: A Union of Human and Faerie Magicians" ~ September 2008, The Year of Freedom," Concept: Synergy, 2008 Audio Recording, Evening Lecture, Meditation.

Lazaris/Pursel, Jach, "Lemuria Revisited: Illuminating Lemurian Nights, Congress of Magicians, September 2008, The Year of Freedom

Magic and Destiny

Barbara Swicegood Fisher

The Beginning—In this Lifetime

I was born in the Piedmont region of North Carolina about nine months after World War II ended, thus ushering in the leading edge of the baby boomers. I am the oldest of four siblings and grew up on an incredibly beautiful dairy farm with lakes, ponds, orchards, pastures, woods, barns, streams, cows, ducks, Guineas, chickens, pigs, horses, etc. As a child, I was very feisty (having red hair), totally at one with the beautiful nature all around, responsible, loved learning, and was wide-eyed and dreamed big. I tried to be a good little Baptist girl, as the church was on our property. So, I spent lots of time in church trying to understand and sort out spiritual stuff. This early and monumental desire to know about spirituality was a huge motivator for my entire life.

Moving ahead, I had a rough and tumble childhood, spending most of my time in trees. A fun thing that all people seem to remember about me as a child was that I was "the little redheaded girl who hung upside down in the pear tree." Yes, 'tis true—I spent so much time hanging from that tree—necessary pondering time.

Then came my "wounding" when I was twelve. It involved moving from this farm and this land that I so loved. This move broke my heart, and I spent the next years in significant grief. After a while, I finally emerged from this pain. I then graduated from an exceedingly small high school, and soon after this, I experienced my first *huge* miracle, and it is from this that I knew without reservation that magic exists.

As stated above, I was part of a huge agricultural family. I had no family money to go to college, but I always knew that I was going. I always prayed and asked God for help. In the summer, prior to the upcoming college year, I received a scholarship that paid for everything for four years to any state supported school. *This scholarship was a magnificent gift of magic that changed my life.*

College was wonderful, as I chose to go to a college located in the upper Blue Ridge Mountains, close to both Tennessee and Virginia. Just like the farm, this land was exquisitely beautiful, and I fell in love once again with nature—the land, trees, rocks, and streams. I was so happy!

After College—Moving to Atlanta, Starting a Career, Meeting My First Husband, and LAZARIS!

Post-graduation, I moved to Atlanta, got a starter job as a Head Start Teacher. I met my first ex-husband, we lived together, smoked a lot of pot, moved to the Georgia countryside, became astrologers, and read Edgar Cayce. This information changed me forever. As I read Edgar Cayce and learned about past lifetimes, I knew with certainty that 1) it was totally true and 2) I wanted a life reading and I wanted it bad.

Moving ahead a few years to April 1976, my then husband was teaching astrology at a progressive university in Carrollton, Georgia (about one and a half hours southwest of Atlanta). A student in his astrology class was attending graduate school and knew someone who had started to do channeling and did *life readings*. This person and his wife had just moved from Michigan to Florida. They were Jach and Peny Pursel. Knowing nothing about the channel, my then husband and I promptly scheduled our first life reading—*it was June 12, 1976*. This is when Lazaris officially entered my life, and my love affair began. My life changed forever.

This reading was the first of many personal readings that I was fortunate enough to have with Lazaris. So many aspects of the beginning readings spoke directly to various parts of me. There was no doubt about the accuracy or depth of this information. I learned that my grandmother (in this life) is one of my counselors and that a Roman lifetime lover is my other counselor. Meeting Lazaris was, and is, unfathomable. I learned about torturous lifetimes, R&R lifetimes, lifetimes with my current husband, powerful almost-going-home lifetimes in

Lemuria, Atlantis, Egypt, and the current world. They all have threads of me—*there was and is no doubt.*

Divorce, Changing Careers, Lazaris and the First Lemurian Wedding

In the early '80s, I and my then husband divorced. The Lazaris Material was so crucial during this grieving process. In the mid-'80s, I met my second husband, and Lazaris gave us information to have the first "Lemurian" wedding ever in this timing. I asked Lazaris to be present at my wedding and, of course, it happened. Lazaris discusses their presence at my wedding in the tape *The Gentle Walk: Step-by-Step Intimacy with Your Higher Self.*[1]

During this timing, I returned to graduate school and got my master's degree and became a therapist. From 2000 on, I specialized in Attachment Disorder Therapy. This specialty has provided an opportunity to do the work of this and other lifetimes. I love working with early (beginning of life) traumatized kids to help them heal. I continue to utilize many Lazaris techniques, as well as quantitative EEG-driven neurofeedback in my therapy practice. I have written and coauthored many articles, served as an expert witness, presented at many national conferences, trained therapists internationally, and coauthored two books—*Moving Through Change with Grace*[2] and *Stuck in the Yuck.*[3] My career has been profound, and I have had the joy of helping a good many folks. (All of this is done with a little help from my friend, Lazaris.)

After eighteen years, the second marriage ended, but never did my love and joy of Lazaris and the material presented. After the divorce, I moved to a small city about five miles from downtown Atlanta. It is an incredibly beautiful community, and I have been involved in local politics, the garden club, lots of community service projects, and am currently heading up a citizen's advocacy committee to reuse, reduce, and recycle single-use plastics. My little city is a wonderful and bountiful place to live, to be, and to grow. It is analogous to all the places that I have loved—the dairy farm as a child, the Blue Ridge Mountains as a college student, and now here, as an adult. All these places are where the Earth loves herself, and this love is apparent in the plants, minerals, animals, and people.

Lazaris Work That I Love

All the material is exquisite! I especially resonate to the work on shame, the faces of the soul, Lemuria/the crystal cities, the Muses, the Guardians, the magical child/the underworld, the Enneagram, Merlin, Arthur and Knights of the Round, and the Archetypes. I love *The Crisis Tape*[4], the *Peace Red Label*[5] meditation, and all the beautiful blendings.

Fortunately, I have attended many international workshops—in Iceland, Lake District, England, Florence, Tuscany, Bali, New Zealand, Spain, and South Africa. These, to simply say it, have all been transformational. During these exquisite times, I have met so many magicians throughout the world, seen fabulous places, been on fun field trips, have loved and been loved deeply by the lands and the folks. So much magic—so much beauty and love.

The last workshop in Cape Town[6] was particularly profound, as I spoke to Lazaris. I had a challenging year in

2018-2019, losing both of my pets and having a huge financial crisis, related to what I think I must pay for freedom (a thread of all my lifetimes). Lazaris gave me such magnificent and helpful information, that basically revealed my impedance in living the dream was forgiveness, and that it was time for me to be more visible—for the world to see who I am. Lazaris stated that my magician friends see who I am. However, I must deal with my fears to consciously step into the dream. I returned from Cape Town and have listened to what Lazaris suggested.

Thus, an already great life was even more impactful, as I know that I cannot retreat into the safety of my ego games— my self-pity, my victimhood, the lesser, the past scripts, etc. These negative ego games got stripped away so that I can be and do what I came to be and do. No excuses anywhere!

This thriving, proactive group of magicians (Friends of Lazaris) indicates my internal changes—of my allowing the beauty, love, visibility, and light to come mightily into my life. I love the group, love the potentials, love the creativity, love the vision, and love being part of such a vibrant community.

Lastly...the Continuing of a Magical Life

I fill my life with so many huge and small miracles present in living a more conscious life, and I have come to expect these. However, I notice and treasure each one—large or small. I am extremely grateful. I have generally turned over my dreams and imagination to my Soul and Higher Self to manifest their dreams for me. I rely on resonant and choice magic, and, if a problem arises, I simply place it into a cauldron of mystery and, about twenty-four hours later, a fabulous solution occurs. I truly live a magical, involved, and compassionate life, filled with great family, friends, pets, activities, nature, and purpose. It is not without issues, as I am a physical being and feel the full gamut of emotions, having to do with loss and pain that everyone else experiences. The major difference for this lifetime is I am coming home, but, prior to my leaving, I am going to be and do all that I can to love, help, and protect Mother Earth.

*Barbara Swicegood Fisher is the creator of two important healing programs, Brain Healing and Heart Healing Resources. Barbara has a bachelor's degree in psychology and political science and a master's degree in counseling psychology. She is the coauthor of two books—*Moving through Change with Grace *and* Stuck in the Yuck. *Both books focus on healing from depression, anxiety, and pain. As well, she has authored and coauthored many articles focusing on healing early childhood trauma that often takes place in the adopted world and is a Reactive Attachment Disorder specialist. She has co-published research regarding neurofeedback, trauma, and healing. She is an international speaker, presenter, and therapist. More importantly, Barbara is a metaphysician, an astrologer, a healer, a cosmic and spiritual advisor, who has studied all over the world to learn about resonance, abundance, health, manifestation, divine healing, and transformative awareness of "Creating our own Reality" by blending science and spirituality. Growth, healing, compassion,*

love, and service to humankind have always been at the forefront of her life and work.

Endnotes:

[1]Lazaris/Pursel, Jach, "The Gentle Walk: Step-by-Step Intimacy with Your Higher Self," Concept: Synergy, 1989, Audio Recording.

[2]Swicegood, Barbara, MS, Lpc, Turber, Janice, Med Lpc, "Moving through Change with Grace," Outskirts Press, Paperback, 2007.

[3]Swicegood, Barbara, MS, Lpc, Turber, Janice, Med Lpc, "Stuck in the Yuck of Depression, Anxiety, Abuse and Trauma. A Book for Healing," Outskirts Press, Paperback, 2013.

[4]Lazaris/Pursel, Jach, "The Crisis Tape, Accelerated Journey Series," NPN Publishing, Concept: Synergy, 1992, Audio Recording, Meditation.

[5]Lazaris/Pursel, Jach, "Happiness + Peace," Lazaris Red Label Series, Concept: Synergy, 1998, Audio Recording, Meditation.

[6]Lazaris/Pursel, Jach, "Embraced by the Eternal: Unfolding the Lost Secrets of Grace," Concept: Synergy, 2019, PPV Event.

A Surprise Communion with Soul & Spirit

Adrián Orozco Blair

A recognition and awakening to the presence of my masculine and feminine divine, Spirit and Soul.

I t was a warm spring day in my room of wood trim and the big windows on the second floor of an old house. The windows opened to an exuberantly green-leaved maple tree. I lived in this beautiful room, part of a large home with housemates. I had moved to the San Francisco Bay Area from Mexico six years prior. I came to the Bay to become a healer of sorts, not knowing how that would look.

During the first year in the Bay, I found that, while I had a powerful ability to connect with my spirituality, I spent most of my time disconnected from my body and emotions. Finding myself with this hurdle, I moved toward becoming a psychotherapist, emphasizing the use of theater tools and other body processes to wake myself up emotionally and physically. I was committed to awakening to greater spontaneity and aliveness.

The experience I am about to share happened six months before completing my seven-year schooling journey towards becoming a psychotherapist.

My romantic partner lived in Southern California. We would regularly have deep-sharing video-call conversations while away from each other physically. We were on one of these calls, and she shared that she was in a kind of crisis regarding her sense of reliability and self-confidence at her work. As I listened, I started to notice images coming into my mind. These images had a life of their own beyond mimicking what she was sharing. They came accompanied by a glowing warmth in my chest and a tickling excitement in my breath. I listened until I found a moment to respond. I then translated what I saw; I saw her working with people. It was an image of her with expansive arms like wings, creating a gentle space where people were shining, unfolding in their nature.

I said, "I see a prowess of yours creating a nest for people to feel safe, welcome, and loved." It was as if this vision helped her connect to strength in her and part of what she experienced as her true nature, bringing a sense of reliability and self-confidence. She thanked me for seeing this in her, giving her clarity and hope.

I am a people person, and I often enjoy vulnerable conversations resulting in experiences of feeling seen. But this…this was different. There was a thrill, an excitement, and a new knowing that came with the visions.

Later that morning, in another call with a friend on the East Coast, I again found myself experiencing a warm and exciting knowing accompanied by an image. I paid closer attention this time, and I noticed a sensation of a column of light coming up the right side of my body from my hip up into my head. A deep and warm smile came over me, in my face and my whole body. I saw images of my friend, where I could see her seeing people in her life and how the quality of her seeing had integrity, a level of nuance and fidelity that created a simultaneous experience of coming into the present moment and transcendence. I adventured to share with my friend what I saw, and she felt deeply seen, understood, and loved.

I shared about the warmth and the visions I had experienced. In explaining it to her, I had another image come to me, but now of myself. I saw myself standing with a valley of light coming out of the front of my body as people were before me. The image came with another knowing. This valley of light was a projector showing me having visions of the love of people that were vulnerable with me. I finished saying this to her, and I felt located. With a lightweight but magnetic feeling, I was in the right place and the right time, joyously acknowledged in pleasure. I was witnessing part of my true nature.

I believe everything that exists is made from the masculine and feminine divine, Spirit and Soul. I interpret states of experience connected to Spirit as quickening, accelerating emotional states, such as effervescent joy. Spirit connects with light in its quickness, piercing, filling spaces with its rays. On the other hand, Soul is about being slow, sensing textures, becoming space, making way for experiences, being the ocean within which life can flourish. This day I was to have lucid experiences of both Soul and Spirit.

That same day another friend came to visit me. She arrived, and we sat in my room. She sat on my bed, and I at my desk. I was brimming with excitement and started sharing, putting together the experiences of that morning. She listened, curious. As I spoke, I expected the excitement from telling this story to begin to wane. I concluded sharing and realized more profoundly I had discovered part of my love. I said this to her, and I went into a state of deep joy. Fireworks of pleasure and significance shot and danced through my body. They tickled me and made me laugh and giggle in high pitch. I was too excited to be self-conscious, and waves of excitement turned into hopping on my chair and clapping with my hands and feet. I kept expecting this joy to come down, but as a fountain, it kept coming! For about ten minutes, I spouted, sung, and shined warmth and joyous exhilaration. My friend was happy, and slightly confused, because of the length of my expression. Then the energy finally began to calm. As my breathing calmed, I began to feel a warm vibration everywhere I sensed, including sight, sound, taste, touch, and smell.

It was oceanic. I was still in an altered state of consciousness. A few moments ago, I could not stop moving and found my body jumping in ways I could not plan. Now, I did not want to move. The slower I became, the more I felt pleasure in sensation and being. I was drawn to textures of foliage, grain of wood, and flat, smooth, rough-looking, white walls. The world around me became more united and cohesive.

I settled into my chair, and every movement of my body was a caress from the inside out. I tried talking, and I stopped. I felt like I was interrupting something sacred. The silence was thick. I lowered my volume, slowed my words, and described my experience to my friend. All was well within and without me.

This oceanic communion lasted for nearly two hours. There had been such a contrast of states that it became clear to me I had been "visited" by my divine feminine, Soul, and divine masculine, Spirit.

What to do after being touched with such grace? I had recognized a part of my love, new to me, and then was visited by these transcendent states of Spirit and Soul. I feel less alone in the world. I live my relationship to the physical world as one that is more enchanted than before. I sense Spirit and Soul more and more, in and around me. In the textures of the tree out my window and the glimmers of light as the wind makes the leaves dance. The pleasure that arises as I slow the pace at which I walk, discovering effortless movement, like sensing the veins and blood that make life happen moment by moment. We and our world are woven by fabrics of these energies, just beneath the surface.

Adrián is a champion for deep relationship, emotional experience and expression, helping more of the World be friends and lovers with more of the World. Originally from San Miguel de Allende, México, Adrián is a psychotherapist with an online private practice, as well as a playback theater actor and facilitator (a community empathy improv theater and music ritual). Adrián loves exploring creativity through music, movement, channeling, and intimate relationships with loved ones and Nature.

My Journey with Lazaris

Sally North

L azaris has been the center of my spiritual life since 1984, when I attended my first weekend seminar. I will always be grateful to Jach Pursel and those of Concept: Synergy who made this possible. Since then, I have spent time processing, programming, praying, attending many events, and listening to tapes and CDs.

At the beginning of my work with Lazaris, I was a lawyer. I used the materials to program results and to help me find and counsel clients. This allowed me to gain more confidence and usually produced great results for me, my clients, and the firm I later joined.

While working for this firm, one case I remember well was Logan v MW Trucking, et al. (Because I can't use the names of former clients or who they sued, the name is fictitious.) The wife of Mr. Logan brought the case on his behalf, as well as his family's. The facts showed that Mr. Logan was gravely injured when a truck came unexpectedly into his lane, colliding with his automobile. He suffered a severe brain injury and crippling injuries. His team of doctors diagnosed his mental state as being that of a child between one and two years old. He was not able to talk or recognize his family. The prognosis was that he would need care for the rest of his life with minimal improvement expected.

The insurance company representing the trucking company claimed the driver and his helper were independent contractors not covered by the trucking company's policy. The driver had some insurance, but not enough to cover the injuries involved or the care required. During the discovery stage, we requested documents from the trucking company. They took us to a warehouse containing documents of the trucking company.

My paralegal and I searched for a day and found nothing tying the driver to the company. The following weekend, I processed, programmed, and prayed to find the important information. We returned on Monday to that warehouse. Within an hour, we located a box with documents naming the driver and the helper as "named insureds" under the company's multimillion-dollar policy. Needless to say, the offer to settle went up dramatically. Although I retired before the final settlement, I learned the case ultimately settled for a substantial amount!

In 1995 my mother passed away. I took a break from practicing law. During that break, with the help of Lazaris and some dear friends, I decided to change professions. I had taught for a short time in Oklahoma after graduating from college. I liked teaching, but, after researching it, I knew I would need a California teaching certificate. Teaching in California would require more school. I found a program offered by Los Angeles Unified School District (LAUSD), the District Intern Program. It would allow me to teach while getting the further classwork they offered. To qualify, I had to pass tests and find a school to hire me. Naturally, I turned to Lazaris for help.

A close friend who goes to Lazaris helped me to make a "Treasure Map," with photos of me and pictures of young children from magazines, interacting in a school setting. I hung the Treasure Map on my bedroom wall. I was accepted into the program and hired to teach a kindergarten/first-grade split.

I loved teaching! However, it wasn't always easy. I was fifty-eight years old, but I had very low seniority. I was one of the last to choose my class, grade, and track at the end of the school year. So, when I retired, I had taught every grade in elementary school. Most years, I had a different grade level, with new textbooks and materials, and I also had to purchase materials, such as books, for the classroom library.

One stressful event occurred in my sixth year of teaching. In the fall of 2008, I got an opportunity to leave my school for one closer to home. A principal contacted me, offering a second-grade class. Perhaps I should have been wary, since a teacher and a substitute had already resigned. But I accepted the new assignment.

Almost immediately, I experienced trouble. After trying several strategies, the children informed me they planned to get rid of me, as they had the other two teachers. I went to my principal for help. The "help" I was given included several written reprimands claiming my teaching was below standards. I hired a lawyer recommended by the teacher's union and was given a transfer.

I later learned that the principal was on probation and retired at the end of that school year. By November of that year, I had two new classes of prekindergarten at a nearby school. That school had low attendance in each session. The principal told me she planned to close PreK at the end of the school year and not offer it the following year.

By the end of that year, I had both sessions filled, and I continued to teach prekindergarten until I retired in 2012. I retired due to a knee problem that interfered with walking. And, of course, I turned to Lazaris to help me decide to retire.

Whenever I face a crisis or have an important decision to make, I listen to tapes like *The Crisis Tape*,[1] *Handling Crisis to Maximize Personal Success*,[2] and many others as appropriate.

I had two successful knee replacement surgeries and can walk, dance, and even jog for exercise. I also had a mastectomy of my left breast for breast cancer in 2017. I did not have chemotherapy or radiation, and still, the cancer has not returned. I used healing tapes, processed, and programmed. I also prayed!

I am so grateful for the help I received from Lazaris, my friends, and my family! Last year my sister Anne died from ovarian cancer in Oklahoma. I was privileged to spend a lot of time with her during her last two years. For much of that time, she felt well, and we had a lot of fun doing activities we loved. Toward the last, she was quite ill. At the insistence of a dear friend from Lazaris, I did a mediation, releasing her to make her best choice: to let go or stay. She chose to leave.

God/Goddess/All That Is, Lazaris, and my seen and unseen friends have comforted me and helped with my grief.

And so, my Journey with Lazaris continues to bring me love, happiness, and success, as well as moments of magic, wonder, and fun!

Sally North lives in an active, vibrant, independent-living senior community in Southern California. She retired from lawyering after twenty-three years and from teaching in elementary school after ten years. Sally enjoys reading, walking, dancing, and "hanging out" with family and friends.

Endnotes:

[1]Lazaris/Pursel, Jach, "The Crisis Tape, Accelerated Journey Series," Concept: Synergy, 1991, Audio Recording, Discussion, Meditation.

[2]Lazaris/Pursel, Jach, "Handling Crisis to Maximize Personal Success," Concept: Synergy, 1999, Audio Recording, Discussion, Meditation.

A COVID Story

Keith Michael Thompson

Thre has been so much fear of late surrounding the new variant of the COVID virus. Further information is shared almost daily in this second summer of the pandemic. The level of confusion and ambiguity it brings can be overwhelming at times. For the most part, people want certainty, and, to have it, they will choose the information that gives them a level of assurance to move forward through these challenging times.

Recently, I found out that I was exposed to COVID in one of the workplaces I frequent. In specific ways, I was not surprised, as I live in Louisiana, one of the places in the US where the vaccination rate is, sadly, low. I'm vaccinated. This fact alleviated some of the fear I felt encroaching me, but not totally.

The emotions I felt moved fluidly from blame and anger to pessimism and frustration. My emotions were partly there because of how I found out about being exposed. I overheard a coworker speaking to another about several employees at home with COVID. I had had contact with one of these individuals three days before.

It took a moment for it to sink in. No one in authority at my workplace had taken the time to inform me. I felt a sense of betrayal and a lack of being valued. It awakened in me an awareness of the complexity of the environment this pandemic has created in our society. Were the owners of the business I worked in responsible for telling me of the potential exposure when they believe that this pandemic is not as severe as the mainstream media says? How should I balance my desire for safety with their desire to operate their business environment as their beliefs dictate?

Our society highly regards freedom of individual choice. People have a right to choose how to protect themselves from this virus. They have a right to act or not to act on information that is given. In many ways, they have the right to trust in the ways that create safety for themselves and those they love and care about. Yet something keeps whispering in my ear to take this deeper. Don't just settle for knowing that everyone has the choice to engage this pandemic in the ways that are right for them. I sat with this.

The beauty of this reflection was that I was conscious of my resonance of feelings. It helped keep me from moving into a state of apathy. I allowed myself to sit with what was there. I allowed myself to be quiet and still. I opened the door to go into the Quiet of Stillness.

Slowly, I felt an awareness seep into my conscious self. It was an awareness I knew and lived in my daily life, but, somehow, it held a different weight of importance. This awareness carried a presence. It was given definition when a friend reminded me that, with freedom comes the responsibility of your impact. This truth held the essence of understanding the ambiguity of what freedom can bring in this particular experience. What is your impact as you exercise your freedom?

I needed to find a more balanced state to sit with this knowing. I heard Lazaris call me to come and be with them. So I did, by going into an impromptu blending. What a gift! A blending is a process by which I allow myself to enter an altered state of consciousness. It is not as deep a state as meditation. I use the concept of my safe place to anchor me in the altered state. My safe place is the place I have created in my mind, where I go to find that sense of safety. When I know that I'm safe, it allows me to explore more freely the experiences the blending will reveal.

As I eased into my safe place, Lazaris was there waiting. They surrounded me in their light, calming the fear I knew I could not quiet. In their light of love, they spoke of compassion and understanding. They reminded me that this was an opportunity to lean upon compassion and allow the mystery of compassion to make a difference in how I could now move forward with this reality.

I just let them love me in as complete a way as I could. When the blending was done, I felt changed. I could not say how, but I knew there was a difference in me.

Some of the people exposed to the virus, along with me, were still in the workspace. I could sense their fear, but rather than acting from anxiety, I found myself working from a place of compassion and understanding. I approached one of my coworkers and asked her if she was vaccinated. She would not answer me, so I asked again. She said she was not and that she would not be vaccinated. I almost moved into anger, but I remembered the understanding. I said, "I respect your reasons for not wanting the vaccine, but from now on I will mask. I am vaccinated, but I can still be a carrier and I want to protect you." I immediately saw her body posture shift into a more comfortable state. Somehow, this opened the door to us having a limited conversation about how the vaccine has protected me. This doesn't mean my coworker will get vaccinated, but it showed me the power of holding compassion and understanding in these powerful times of change.

In all of this experience, I recognized that my coworkers were having an impact on my reality, by expressing their freedom not to be vaccinated. I also recognized that I was having an impact upon them as well. That I could choose to come from a place of anger and blame, or I could cultivate compassion and understanding. This awareness helped me to honor my freedom, as well as theirs.

Keith Michael Thompson has had a love for writing since discovering the power of the English language in his childhood. Growing up in the Bahamas, he learned the King's English from his grandmother, who was a schoolteacher. Keith is certified massage therapist and movement therapist in the tradition of Thomas Hanna. He has had a vibrant practice for thirty-eight years. He is also a visual artist. From photography and talisman making to creating sacred pieces made of both natural and man-made products for gardens, Mr. Thompson's love of beauty has found its way into many people's lives.

Transformation—
A Wise Woman's Journey

Lee Ann Romine

I want to share a little glimpse into how the many facets of the Lazaris Material have been woven into my life through my deeply treasured relationship that I have been blessed to have with Lazaris over the past three decades.

Sitting here now, I can see that girl…raised in a time of free love, but born into a family with deep, scary beliefs revolving around anything that wasn't Jehovah's Witness approved. As deep as the rebellion to anything religious was, the fears ran even more profound. One evening, heading home from my accounting job to get dinner on the table, it hit me. Something that sounded like a loud click.

I had no way of knowing then what that click could mean, but, within a very short time, I found myself abandoned and newly divorced. With a young son, and feeling utterly alone in the world, something kept nagging me as I wended my way through the terrifying and redefining days ahead. I had never—would never—have even considered the idea of stopping into a metaphysical bookstore a few short days before (after all, anything like metaphysics was evil and, most certainly, would take my "everlasting life" away, right??).

You see, "way back" in the late 1980s, the "New Age" was dawning, and "those" kinds of places were popping up all over Phoenix, Arizona, my hometown. I am still in possession of the gift of being the *fool* and jumping off into the unknown, but this time of following that rebel's call was a huge defining moment in my world.

A tiny and out-of-the-way "gift shop" was hiding right next door to the grocery store where I stopped in quite often. Walking in, I was overwhelmed with tchotchkes galore. Cluttered and sparkling gifts everywhere. I took a few steps forward and saw the room open up a bit, and rows of books and crystals filled the back of the space—nothing fancy, just regalia of different subjects and small assortments of new age stuff.

The bookstore owner suggested that I rent the first of the Lazaris tapes. Please understand I had absolutely no idea of what channelling was and was still coming from a place of "demons" around every corner. But the nudge internally was not going to be ignored.

I brought home the VHS tape. I sat on the floor in front of my VCR and TV and pushed the button. Terrified and exhilarated all at once, I was mesmerized immediately by Jach's calm demeanor and, then again, when Lazaris entered…and *bam*! My life pivoted at that moment.

I began a journey of self-discovery, truth-finding, and healing that has been the basis of my life since that day. I ended up quitting a lucrative accounting job and started working at that bookstore that same year. While working at the bookstore, I connected with my future husband and one of my dearest friends. I learned to meditate, manifest, heal and even do psychic readings along the way. As I grew into my spirituality's strength, I realized the real meaning of being a "magician" is all about. For me, the term is multifaceted, but the overarching truth is that we each create our own reality. Every bit of that reality. We create, or we allow. That's power. True power. You see, from that perspective, no one else ever has power over you! You become the magician as you learn to weave together the truths and understand how to do so consciously.

Like many in the 1980s, I was searching for more, searching for truth, searching for understanding and meaning. It was in the tiniest of moments, and in the cracks and crevices of my day, where I found the most magic.

The one constant has been Lazaris and the truths and techniques I learned watching those first videos. I create my own reality. I *create* my own reality. I *create my own reality*!

Life is a gift. Ours is to learn to receive!

Twenty years later, these tenets held me together through a devastating decade, where I allowed depression and anxiety to take over my days. I moved across the country and lost myself. However, through that dark time, I found an even deeper appreciation and love for my friend Lazaris. Please set aside any preconceived notions about what "spirituality" *should* look like. One of the most valuable lessons I have learned is that judging pretty much destroys our ability to see truth.

I spent an entire decade hiding in one room of my beautiful Victorian home. Why? That's a multifaceted question. On the physical plane, I was debilitated by a chemical imbalance in my brain. Depression and anxiety became my prison. Did that make me less of a mapmaker? I don't see it that way at all. Could I have made healthier choices? Maybe. Was there a purpose? Most definitely.

You see, since time and space are only an illusion, I can pick up where I left off reasonably quickly. And that is what I have done. I have not just picked up where I left off but incorporated all of the treasures learned, and the nuances gathered to weave together what I see now as an integral part of the "why I am" in this life.

Learning to consciously create reality is an ongoing and beautiful part of any magician's plate, and, for me, it has been filled with glimpses of faerie and many forms of "other." As a psychic, medium, and empath, my world is a continual source of wonder and never ceases to amaze me with the breadth of diversity available on so many levels. Diversity in us as humans, through to the varied and constant we know as our crystalline sisters and brothers, to what we consider alien, other dimensions, and more. It is a beautiful experience to watch as others meld, blend, and pick and choose what they will weave with. I'm a watcher; I experience and "see" through the eyes of ancient wisdom and innocent frailty at the same time. As the year 2020 is coming to a close, I can see that we have, as a collective, chosen to learn, grow and experience the birthing pains together. In some ways, I find that a beautiful thing. That no matter how separate we all can be, we choose to evolve together, even if it plays out as a painful pandemic that, in essence, has separated us more than ever. The irony is sweet.

As we sit at the pinnacle of the world becoming new, as was introduced so many years ago in a glimpse in one of the Lazaris tapes (I can't remember which), I realize that their guidance, understanding, care, and knowledge has been the glue and the light that has gotten me to this pivotal point in our world. The world needs us as magicians. Each of us plays an integral part in ushering in the New World. All of us who have been touched by the Lazaris Material and/or have been able to build a vibrant friendship with Lazaris are, in my experience, being called to stand tall and shine bright, with our imaginations sharp, and wills strong, to weave that New World.

In my vision, I see myself walking one step at a time off the edge of reality. As I hold my breath and focus my will and imagination, the fabric builds below me. Thin at first, and filmy, but, then, as my foot touches that fabric, it explodes with thoughts and feelings, choices, decisions, attitudes, and beliefs, and the most brilliant kaleidoscope begins to whirl. I have shifted my success cube into a more robust and fluid rhombus, and I'm off and flowing in a new realm.

As a visionary, I have been honored to witness many do that very same thing. Each person in their beautiful cadence. Some of us still breakdance along happily, and others soar on wings born of a million whispers. But we each are vital and welcome.

One of my dearest legacies is bringing in and raising two beautiful magicians and, so far, two grandchildren, who, without a formal understanding of the Lazaris techniques, have been raised to use those tools in ways that are most magical. I know we have set in motion a new generation that is more than we can even imagine. That "more" is going to be necessary to carry our world forward. As I understand what I am "seeing," infinite versions of our future hang here. In my sight, almost like the old swings made of rope and a board suspended from a limb. Myriads of them swaying gently for the most part. They light up and shiver as our energy grazes them. Hop on for a moment and feel if that one is in alignment with your choices? Yes? Sit and swing, allowing the motion to weave more. If that swing is not just right, then just move along.

For you see, there is no right or wrong choice. Only preference. Yes! We have arrived at that beautifully exhilarating space—creating from pure preference. I ask you—yes, you, the beautifully battered, strong, and remade magician—what is your preference?

Make that choice every day. As you get familiar and comfortable, begin to consciously create every hour, minute, second until it's a natural and automatic thing. Creating every bit of your reality, and then some, is our natural state of being. Creating consciously is, however, a choice and a talent that we grow.

May we all happily move forward with that energy—carrying that responsibility with a smile and maybe just a bit of fear. As you read the words, what speaks to your soul?

The hope and wonder or the truth and triumph? I have a feeling that the very act of reading this now is a clue to your own story, either beginning or scaling up to the next octave of becoming the one that creates their own reality consciously.

I now work in a global arena, teaching, sharing, and guiding entrepreneurs with those same techniques and knowledge. Being a shining light to illuminate your path is my passion. I know that, for my soul, the experiences that I have allowed and created in my life led me to the depth of understanding it would take to help usher in the "New World" that is birthing here in this time and place.

We each create our own reality. Life is a gift, shine bright, and lead with integrity. As I grow my business and share what I know to be true, it is my deepest wish that each of us shares the beautiful spark of a myriad of lights we all love. Thank you, my dear, dear friend, Lazaris. Thank you for being there every moment and sharing the truth so readily for us to share with our world!

Lee Ann Romine lives in a beautiful oak-filled property in rural West Virginia with her husband and fellow magician Robert. She spends her days as Transformational Business coach, Psychic and Theta Healer. She is enjoying a rewarding and happy life, alongside her family and friends, while sharing her wisdom and knowledge with those who are open to becoming more of who they chose to be, as they find their most aligned and abundant path.

Peaceful Mind

Mary Woodhouse

After years of ladder climbing, years of balancing work, income and family, after reaching what were likely to be my best professional title and highest salary by far, it all vanished in an instant. I was unemployed for two and a half years during the Great Recession, losing my job soon after the stock market plunge, the beginning of the global financial crisis, in late September 2008. I turned fifty while I was unemployed. A startling reality at the time.

We sat in his black Audi sedan, on an October afternoon, in a parking lot. We faced a wall of the vast cinder-block industrial building recently transformed into a snazzy, hip, product design office. My colleague, my boss, my friend, Allen, told me the new division could not survive this sudden change in the economy. He had recruited me. I joined only five months earlier. I was laid off along with thirty other coworkers. As a magician who works with Lazaris, and a person who embraces the New Age-based belief, "you create your own reality," this personal and world crisis threw me into a period of emotional intensity, reflection, meditation, healing and magic.

During my time being unemployed, I was often completely freaked out. Paralyzed with fear, it felt physical at first, a sense of shock mixed with terror. I leaned upon my work with Lazaris to bring relief, insight, change, and healing. Working with Lazaris Material meditations, techniques and concepts is part of my everyday life. Working with any of the material is essentially learning to work with myself as a spiritual being, to discover resources, friends, even worlds, within.

The Great Recession was a tough time for a multitude of people. Our little family hunkered down and managed. My wife, Sarah, self-employed, was able to increase her caseload. I was grateful each time the unemployment benefits were extended by Congress. Our son was in sixth grade. I became the homemaker mom instead of the breadwinner mom. I cherished spending more time with my son. Sarah was steadfast in her commitment and support, compassionate through my ups and downs. We weathered this difficult time together and came out of it stronger, closer.

A major reprieve during my unemployed years was a temporary position at one of the largest financial services firms in the world, which is based in Boston and has many large campuses, one in rural Massachusetts. My temporary workplace was a fancy new, environmentally friendly designed office building.

Perhaps because of my continued state of freak out, I was drawn to the Red Label Meditation set *Happiness + Peace*.[1] I sure needed that. I wanted to be happy, not freaked out. I asked myself, can I actually get to a state of peace? What does a state of peace even mean?

Here is the description of the Red Label Series from Concept: Synergy:

> "The Red Label Series is a very special series of meditations from Lazaris. Each title contains two topics which work together, and for each Lazaris gives a days-on/days-off formula for listening which follows the pattern with which your subconscious works most effectively in creating change. Though they are not subliminal recordings, once you have listened to them consciously, many may be used at night while you're asleep. Each title consists of two 30-minute meditations."[1]

In the Happiness meditation, Lazaris says, "to be happy, one must achieve a peaceful state of mind."[2] This assertion astounded me and captured my imagination. Well, isn't to *be happy* one of my major goals in life? Isn't that what my parents wanted for me, and what I want for my son? Isn't that one of the founding principles of our nation? The pursuit of happiness? If I *must* achieve a peaceful state of mind to *be happy*, well then, dammit, I'd better put the pedal to the metal and get focused.

So, I followed the directions on the tape series, meditated with the days-on/days-off pattern. I usually listened in an awake state, but, since it was okay to listen while sleeping, I didn't worry if I fell asleep or drifted off. In Lazaris meditations, we often find ourselves walking in a beautiful natural environment: in the woods, on a beach, meandering through a garden, moving up a mountain path, and so forth. These two meditations started out in that way, then guided me to wondrous inner locations with a combination of beautiful imagery of a natural environment, leading to esoteric personal encounters, experiences, symbolism, and metaphors.

Back at the global financial services firm, back in 2010, my first experience of a mental shift due to the *Happiness* + *Peace* meditations came during an ordinary moment. Perhaps I was in my office cube or walking downstairs to the gourmet cafeteria with its many food stations. I noticed a period of time when I had no thoughts going through my head. A quiet in my mind, a pause in my stream of consciousness. What? No thoughts? Is it possible to have no thoughts? Accompanying the period of no thoughts, was a sense of pleasant calm. I experienced a time of simple sensory receiving of sights, sounds and movement. Is this it? Is this my peaceful state of mind gaining ground? Am I getting there?

Yes, I was getting there. The periods of "no thought" became more frequent and lasted longer. I liked the experience of a quieter mind. My more peaceful mind allowed mental space for me to receive the sensory experience of the present moment. I received the present more consciously and pleasurably; the sights, the sounds around me were more pleasantly alive. I received people more, the sight of them, the pleasure of eye contact, the words they were speaking. By receiving the present more, I became more present.

A great benefit of this work was that I eventually became aware of the actual thoughts moving through my mind. I became consciously aware of patterns, of different types of thought moving through my head and feelings associated with many of those thoughts.

The long-term effect is I have slowly become a completely conscious thinker. This is a fascinating personal accomplishment. Because I am a conscious thinker, I am fully aware of every word going through my head. What an amazing shift in my experience of myself. I've found new approaches to active thinking, and still experience periods of peaceful "no thought."

Thinking is such an intimate personal component of our individuality. In our spiritual work, we learn that thinking is connected to the Unseen, and is part of the mysterious process of reality creation. We experience our thoughts as private and separate from all else. But, in the great oneness, our personal thoughts and feelings, beliefs and attitudes, choices and decisions flow as participants in some mysterious dance, creating possibilities, probabilities, and the actualities we eventually experience. So, thinking plays its part in the magic of reality creation. Awareness of my thinking is empowering. It allows me the freedom to choose what and how I think.

Two examples of the thought patterns I became aware of are what I refer to as *morning kitchen negative thinking* and *incessant 'splainin'*.

Early in the morning, I often load or unload the dishwasher, pick up the kitchen, all mindlessly, in a sleepy haze. I became aware of my repetitive negative thought pattern. I would have thoughts complaining to myself about my wife. Picky little negative thoughts, complaining silently to myself, about her lack of cleaning up the kitchen, which led to a number of inner explanations of the issue at hand and the exploration of additional perceived shortcomings.

I became aware of this repetitive pattern of thought, and how unkind it was. With this awareness, I suddenly felt deeply sad I was treating the love of my life this way in my head, unbeknownst to her. I recognized how it was a lazy, intrusive, automatic thinking. Becoming aware of these thoughts, I could see I previously perceived them as thoughts that didn't matter, didn't hurt anyone. Private thoughts, secret even. I actually hadn't been aware of these thoughts enough to even categorize them until this new awareness of my thinking.

In a flash, I could see how these thoughts did matter. They encouraged, within myself, a mental area of holding a negative view of my dear wife. It could affect my subsequent tone of voice, body language and the tone of my gaze when greeting her when she woke up. This habit of thinking and its effects were more than unkind, they could be damaging. I began to work on shifting those thoughts, and eventually stopped the repetitive, unloving, inner habit. When I recognized the unkind, negative, repetitive thoughts, I became able to stop them and then consciously chose to think in repetitive affirmations instead. Repeating phrases, which varied. "I love Sarah and Sarah loves me," was one. Others included, "I now have a peaceful state of mind" or "I am happy, I allow myself to be happy" or "I am awake, alive and happy." I would remind myself all the other chores and responsibilities Sarah took care of that I didn't—picking up other rooms in the house, mowing the lawn and many more. So, now I can catch myself, stop any insidious, lazy, negative train of thought, and redirect my thinking to something more beneficial to myself and our relationship. I don't condemn myself for my negativity. I don't fear my negative thinking. I just recognize it and redirect.

Another pattern I became aware of was my *Lucy & Desi's 'splainin'* pattern. I imagine Desi Arnaz saying to Lucy in his thick Cuban accent, "Lucy, let me 'splain it to you." This was my relentless thought pattern of constantly explaining to myself why things were the way they were or what was going on. In becoming aware of this pattern, I could see how much I was trying to figure it all out, but not with conscious focus. My explanations often had a negative slant and no depth. This was a shallow, throw away, unconscious flow of repetitive, rote explanations, often deciding unilaterally what other people's motives and personal issues were. This was an unexamined, again, habitual flow of thought from my Negative Ego. Don't get me started.

Morning kitchen negative thinking and Desi Arnaz 'splainin'-to-Lucy thinking were the two major unconscious thought patterns I became aware of and changed following my work with the *Happiness + Peace* Red Label Meditations. I return to the series often, though not in the days-on, days-off pattern. Sometimes, I let it run on very low volume while I work. In time, the substitute habit of repetitive-affirmation thinking took hold in a new way. Now, if I drop into a mindless unconscious thinking, rather than rote negativity, I *automatically* drop into an underlying phrase, such as "I am awake, alive and happy," "I allow happiness," "I am loving and loved" or "I love life and life loves me." Rote positivity! The incessant stream-of-consciousness explaining has also stopped. I can think about something deeply, by choice, but if the incessant shallow explaining turns on, I am able to recognize it is happening, say to myself, "Oh I'm doing that thing where I try to explain everything. I don't have to do that," and just stop. I may fall into automatic affirmations, or just return to the present with a sense of "no thought."

A few months after my temporary position ended, I took the first job someone offered me, accepting a lower-level position in the marketing department of a small financial organization in the Northeast. I slowly climbed a rung of the ladder again and feel good about the position I currently hold. I'll soon be reaching my tenth year. I have worked with lots of other Lazaris Material processes and meditations over the years to focus on additional areas that capture my interest in this grand journey of personal spiritual growth.

I have achieved a peaceful state of mind. I continue to reap the benefits every day. Because of this spiritual work, I am able to experience the pleasure of presence, awareness that allows choice, rote positivity, and a wonderful, loving relationship. Life isn't perfect; there are plenty of challenges. I am happy.

Mary Woodhouse lives in New England and works in a financial institution marketing department. *Mary relishes interesting creative projects that tickle her fancy, such as the development of this anthology with community members.* *Another fulfilling project was authoring the pamphlet,* A Fan's Guide to Jane Roberts—author of the Seth books—Saratoga Springs. *A third creative project was the invention of the SpiritCradle® Rocking Meditation device and small-group healing circle method.* *Mary enjoys cooking, gardening, genealogy, spending time with family and friends as well as unraveling the mysteries of the universe.*

Endnote:

[1]Lazaris/Pursel, Jach, "Happiness + Peace," Lazaris Red Label Series Concept: Synergy, 1998, Audio Recording, Meditation.

The Magic of Lazaris' Love

Kathy Tountas

I became a Bride of Christ when I was seven years old. That's what they called us when we made our first communion. Not many years later, I decided I wanted a divorce. Christ had been ignoring my prayers. It became official when I told my parents I would not be going to a Catholic high school. I admit this was intended to be a snappy joke, an attempt to sound as if I came away untouched by it all. But I'm getting ahead of myself.

The first half of my life was filled with painful memories, and they began early. I was born to a woman who had five children, two boys and three girls. She didn't want her daughters. My first memory is particularly vivid: my mother leaning over my crib, her face mere inches from mine. I felt her hatred and froze.

"Why don't you die...why don't you just die?"

During my childhood, I fell into the pattern of seeking my mother's love and alternately fearing it. She was different than the mother of my friends, a brother and sister who lived across the street. I don't ever remember a time when my mother got out of bed in the morning to fix me breakfast or prepare lunch for me to take to school. I knew that the mother of my playmates did, because she would call them home to eat when we were deep in a game of softball on Saturdays. It made me sad.

I have a humiliating memory of sitting at my desk in school with fifty-nine other classmates. My attention drifted from what Sister Martha Mary was saying. I looked over at Margaret, who sat beside me one row over. Margaret got straight A's. She was beautifully cared for, hair sleek and shining, always prepared for school, always clean. I was not cared for. I looked down at my own hands, dirt caught in the lines between my thumb and index finger, and hated myself.

My mother terrified me. She knew how to keep me off balance. She would sometimes reach out and pinch me or slap my face, leaving me confused and yearning to know how I had offended her. Too often, I was on the receiving end of beatings from her with my father's leather belt, administered with the words, "This is for your own good."

During one such beating, I remember feeling like a caged animal as she backed me into a corner. In that moment, I realized all of my feelings had turned to hate. I think I was about ten years old, but I don't remember what I did to deserve her retribution. I licked my wounds and eventually came out of my room.

When I looked at her, I couldn't stop thinking, "I hate you…I hope you die."

Her eyes ominously dark, she stared at me for the longest time before she said, "One of these days I'll be gone, and then you'll be sorry."

Without missing a beat, I immediately thought, *No, I won't!* Even though it was just a thought, it filled the room.

By the time I was around eleven, I was so weighted down with shame and feeling so alone, I gave up. As I lay in bed one night crying, I imagined the peace and silence I was sure to find in a tomb. I wanted to die, and begged God to make it so, but once again my prayer went unanswered.

I was a spiritual seeker from the time I made my first communion, and I craved a personal relationship with God. In spite of my unanswered prayers, I carried the promise of such a relationship as expectancy in my heart.

I remember the exact moment I woke up, when my soul moved within me. I remember the time of day, even the room I was in. It was an afternoon of a weekday, my sons were in school, my husband at work, and I stood in front of my computer in my library looking around somewhat confused. All of a sudden, I spoke in a voice slightly detached, "I have to go home to Goddess. I don't know who my God is, but I'm sorry, I can't be with you. I belong to Goddess." And, in that moment, I felt a warm and attentive response that I knew was God, but I didn't care…I waited for the gift I knew Goddess had for me.

I took part in full moon ceremonies with a group of women, collected books about Goddess; studied ancient cultures, goddess cultures, as I earned a bachelor's degree in anthropology/archaeology; and I visited a local metaphysical bookstore regularly. The first time I heard about the concept of a Higher Self, I was filled with joy. We made attempts to connect with each other, but, because I didn't trust myself or my undeveloped psychic abilities, our relationship developed slowly.

One day I had an urge to visit the metaphysical bookstore. The urge was insistent. I was drawn to the Lazaris Interviews, Books I[1] and II.[2] I picked one up and felt something respond inside of me. I took the books home, went up to my bedroom, closed the door and sat down to read.

As I opened to the first page, I felt Lazaris' warm and loving attention. He knew I was aware of him. It was the first time feeling such a clear connection with my inner world. Everything was changing moment by moment.

Lazaris' explanation of God/Goddess/All That Is, his reference for the Divine, fit into my concept of how I wanted my spirituality to work. It was practical, and that appealed to me, as if it had been created just for me. I knew the bookstore also rented the Lazaris videos. I felt an undeniable desire to return to the bookstore.

It was the middle of the day, and I was alone. My sons wouldn't be home for several hours. Nervously, I took a video home. Every act, every step, seemed of momentous importance. As if my life were somehow on the line. I slipped the heavy tape into the VCR and waited. Jach, Lazaris' channel, introduced himself, and a feeling I now recognize as dread surfaced—that fear that I was about to lose my life, that nothing would ever be the same. It was the video where Lazaris looked directly through the camera into your heart and said, "Do you think you are watching this video by accident? There are no accidents."

He said something else, but the words didn't register with me, because I was sobbing, taken by both joy and anger. And I lashed out at him. "What took you so long? I waited and waited for you. I've waited my whole life for you!"

In those moments, I recognized without any doubt that Lazaris was the promise I held in my heart. Still watching me, I heard him say, "So, if you are willing to do the work…" and motioning with his fingers, urge me to him…"come on, come on!"

And our work together began.

Not long after, Lazaris took me to what I perceived was the center of my universe, and said into the deep silence, "We would never let Kathy believe she was alone." And, from that moment, he has never left me. This commitment to me, and his companionship, fills me with an unending joy. For many years, I would turn to him, weeping, overwhelmed with gratitude that he walked with me on my journey.

Lazaris' love is revelatory in its impact. It didn't take long for me to realize that I wanted to love like Lazaris does. His love is tender and caring. It nurtures and fulfills and is full of sensation. And it is felt on so many levels. These are not just words, but actual feelings identifiable as tenderness and care.

Around that time, a memory surfaced in a night dream, and, in the morning, I awoke with a strange feeling of completeness, satisfaction, as if some ancient desire had been fulfilled. I remember sitting on a sofa waiting for what, I didn't know, but waiting with expectancy.

A man came. He exuded feelings, sensations that wrapped around me, fulfilling me, and at the same time initiating a fine and clear sense of intrigue. He seemed to be my age, blond-white hair, quite refined and beautiful, almost displaying feminine qualities, not outwardly, but in his manner. It was love and caring and gentleness…a strange gentleness that drew me closer in spite of my initial feeling of distaste, which I later realized was a reflection of my own chauvinism.

I felt all of this in a moment, and then he said, "Well, well, well, there you are!"

He seemed to know me, sure enough. He sat beside me. I felt so safe with him. Also, he had such a sense of humor that was quite masculine, with self-assurance. He was an uncommon blend of these qualities at such a deep level. I'd never met anyone like him before.

I said, "Hi! Are you looking for me?"

"Why, yes! And here you are, waiting for us."

"I am?" I looked inward and discovered something returned that had been lost, a feeling of excitement, of reward, a meeting that fulfilled me in a strange way. Yet I knew, too, it was a new beginning.

I asked, "Why have you been looking for me?"

"Why, to bring you home, of course."

I was filled with wonder. "Home?"

"Your Higher Self told us about you, how wonderful you are. And we wanted to see you for ourself. Indeed, we did." His voice was a smile bubbling over with love. It made me happy. It made me laugh out loud.

He said, "May we touch you?"

"Of course," I replied.

He reached over and touched my third eye, and I was filled with a dreaminess, and my eyes closed on their own. He touched my heart, and I was flooded with a tender and encompassing love. I rather leaned forward and felt myself wrapped in a delicious safety. Even now, as I remember, I am filled with the silkiness of that love, awed by the incredible tenderness and care. At the time, I forgot to ask who he was. Later, of course, I realized that he was Lazaris.

With the birth of my two sons, I discovered that my childhood had not prevented me from being able to love. It came from a choice, a promise I made to myself when I was still a child. I remember it was initiated by feeling unloved, which dropped me into a depth created by deep despair. "When I grow up and have children of my own, they will always know that I love them." And I imagined holding a child in my lap and tenderly caring for him. I spoke and felt this promise with unusual intensity. And when I grew up and had my sons, I loved them. I was enraptured by the gift that they were...I lived for them. But it wasn't until Lazaris came into my life that I came to learn that I was loveable. I learned about and felt a depth of love that was unimaginable to me.

As it turned out, and as I knew from the moment I saw them on that ancient VCR, Lazaris was the answer to my prayers.

Kathy Tountas is a mystic, metaphysician and loves working with crystals. She is also a channel, giving voice to cosmic beings, with a special emphasis on Angelic beings, and she paints Angels for people who want a closer connection to this loving guidance. Besides writing and painting, Kathy loves working in her garden and chatting with the nature spirits where they live with her in Michigan; but she feels a special joy anytime she is with her grandchildren.

Endnotes:

[1]Lazaris/Pursel, Jach, "Lazaris Interviews Book I," Concept: Synergy, 1988, Book.

[2]Lazaris/Pursel, Jach, "Lazaris Interviews Book II," Concept: Synergy, 1988, Book.

What Crystals Told Me

Carole Sainte-Marie

When an ordinary person opens his mind and heart, things can become magical. As you are expecting to be told an unusual story, something kept secret until now, I can affirm that your wish will be granted.

It happened during a seminar led by Lazaris in 2003. Words cannot describe properly the profound, intense, and sometimes ecstatic experiences or discoveries that can emerge from a gathering around an ethereal fire burning across time and space, in mythic Lemuria or Atlantis. As well, an incursion in the World of Other, or Fairyland for the young at heart, brings its own share of magic and wonder. The only prerequisite is some faith in their existence as, in truth, anyone could join the circle and live the adventure. However, referring to the allusion of a parade, some actively participate in it, some are simply happy to watch it, while others do not even know that bands and floats are marching on Main Street. Thus, how do you narrate the excitement, the colors, the atmosphere of such a joyful event after it took place? Likewise, how do you describe soul-stirring experiences like remembering your love for the Goddess, fairy friends, and crystals? How can simple human words convey what happened during those seminars and explain the healing or changes that followed? Consequently, the story I promised to tell is of a different nature, although still part of the enchantment of that special event.

I remember quite precisely the long line of tables offering an exceptional display of magnificent, voluminous, and luminous Ancient Ones crystals awaiting their new guardians. I became particularly attracted by a glorious one bearing the title of Wall of Truth. As it was the most majestic crystal I had ever seen, I immediately fell in love. I wanted to bring it back home, and it did not matter that I could not afford it, really. Instead, I juggled with ways to give it my name.

Lazaris spoke brilliantly, as usual. During the presentation, he invited us to ponder, during the interlude, about a fact, problem, or question relating to each of us personally. Having the purchase of the crystal in mind, I sensed a strong pull to go to the Wall of Truth and, even though there were people around me, I put my forehead on its apex. Then, the most incredible thing happened: it spoke to me. "I am not meant to be under your guardianship" were hard words to swallow, as I was so enamored with it. I was feeling so disappointed and disoriented that I wondered how I could enjoy the rest of a seminar that had just begun.

The event resumed and I returned to my seat located among the last rows, by the wall. At lunchtime, I decided to exit the room without giving a glimpse at selling tables. I only had walked a few steps when I suddenly sensed the need to stop right where I was, my right foot still suspended in the air. A crystal was calling me. Puzzled, I approached the table, intuitively knowing where the call had originated. She was an imposing Grandmother, a Magician's Comfort and Healing crystal, and a Purveyor of Truth as well. I gave her an admiring look and, at her silent invitation, I let my hand caress her cold body. All I can say is that my distress was instantly healed, replaced by a serene acceptance of what was.

I went on with the event, my mind free of attachment, but not of the admiration I was having for those two majestic crystals. I waited until the last day to look for a souvenir. Now, what was this citrine that I had never noticed before, sitting at the other end of the tables? Sure, its volume was more modest than the two Ancient Ones I had already encountered, but its radiance was majestic. Intrigued, I read its presentation paper only to find that it possessed a title that awoke something in me. I was standing in front of a Mystic Mills Anchor/Anvil. Mystic Mills? I found this fascinating. However, no matter how beautiful this piece was, I left it there, purchasing material relating to crystals instead.

Back home, days and weeks went by, and I realized I could not forget the citrine. However, this time, I was to act more wisely. As I already had the desire to become the guardian of an Ancient One, I dreamt and envisioned that the right companion would come to me. I used the meditation included in the *Crystals: The Power & Use*[1] and *Crystals: Tools to Co-Creation*[2] cassettes I had bought.

About two years later, another occasion to attend a seminar presented itself. Strolling by the selling tables, I immediately recognized the citrine. The man working at the table, witnessing the encounter, told me that both Dear One—the name that instantly came to my mind—and I became suddenly more luminous. It was now time to open my wallet.

From the moment I had heard or saw the expression Mystic Mills, even though I did not know what it was all about, I sensed the profound desire to take part in such an experience. It became a goal to achieve during this lifetime, something close to an obsession. My new crystalline partner had already been living with me for a few months when I finally received his "biography," channeled by Jach, the person lending his voice to Lazaris. And there it was: our very first meeting, in the land of Lemuria, had happened upon the platform of a Mystic Mill... It became imperative to practice this ancient magical ritual, to reconnect with the power born of intention, to rekindle my partnership with the Elements, to occupy my due place in the Universe. I am a mapmaker, standing between the Old and the New World.

***

Such a fairy tale could have remained secret. But, as things unfolded, I came to read the fascinating book written by Jach about ancient crystals and their former guardians.[3] Inspired by it, and by what transpired from my crystal's biography, and having literary creation as a hobby, I later sensed the need to immortalize my beloved one. Dear One became Dirwön, a spelling that seemed to suit him better because of his old age, and because our modern languages were not in use in Lemuria or Atlantis. I imagined his transmission from one guardian to the other, through eras and civilizations, reincarnated souls reuniting around him. This way, Dirwön is doubly in my heart: as a beautiful shining companion and as a novel.

Learn more about Carole Sainte-Marie on page 26.

Endnotes:

[1] Lazaris/Pursel, Jach, "Crystals: The Power and Use," Concept: Synergy, Audio Recording, Discussion & Meditation,1985.

[2] Lazaris/Pursel, Jach, "Crystals: Tools to Co-Creation," Concept: Synergy, Audio Recording, Discussion & Meditation,1998.

[3] Pursel, Jach, "The Grand Awakenings of Ancient Crystals," Book, 1st Edition, NPN Publishing, 2003.

My First Healing with Lazaris

Janis Rosen

I like my new house on Campbell Street in North River Heights. It stands on a wide street, lined on either side with beautiful old elm trees. My city has the largest urban elm forest in the world.

I'm renting the house from a woman who lives up north, and I am in charge of the place, making decisions on repairs, paint colors and managing it. It's the closest I've come to a sense of ownership and home. Good practice, as my next move will be to buy my own home.

At the age of thirty-seven, I am independent and safe for the first time in my adult life, with no responsibilities for anyone but me, having just liberated myself from a bad marriage. I left with my two cats and with what I came into it with.

I don't have much in the way of furniture, but I don't need much. I buy a waterbed with a wooden frame and headboard and some nice side tables and lamps. I set up the second bedroom as my office space where I see clients. In this first year of independence, I begin to work deeply with Lazaris and the material. I encounter my first crystals, who come into my keeping. Once a week, I see my counselor for a therapy session. I need to understand *why*. I begin to work my way through my life story, remembering and putting it together from a new perspective. I have many insights and understandings about my life and how I got to this juncture in my thirties. They worked well in conjunction with the Lazaris material.

I give myself a year of solitude, to take myself apart and put myself together again. A quiet year to do my inner work and healing with Lazaris and my Higher Self, without impediments, pressure or distractions. I take a new name. In the second year, I begin to make my way back to the world and connect with people.

A few months after my move to Campbell Street, having settled into a new life and a new routine, I have a dream.

It's morning and I am in my bed. Lazaris comes into my bedroom, stands at the foot of the bed, and says, "We are going to heal your knees." This cold pain in both knees has continued to dog and harass me for over a year now. Lazaris stands at the foot of the bed and instructs me to lay on my stomach and look at the headboard. It's my same wooden headboard, but now it's covered with simple, beautiful carvings.

Just as Lazaris is about to begin, one of Lazaris' students comes in to make plans with them for lunch together. I overhear them and get secretly jealous and mad that they are making plans in my bedroom and not inviting or even acknowledging me! I want to go too! The student leaves and Lazaris turns back to me. I pretend I am okay, but I am stewing and seething inside.

Lazaris takes my left foot and pushes a powerful energy through the sole of the foot, which moves with strong momentum up my body and out the top of my head. As this energy moves through me, I am filled with awful feelings of anger and jealously, which ride the momentum and leave through the top of my head. It happens quickly and, once done, all is quiet, within and without.

Lazaris turns to my right leg and says, "This should have been done a long time ago!"

Issues with my right knee began when I was two and a half years old, the year my brother, Marshall, was born, and I was displaced. All the attention from family and friends that had been mine, was now focused on my new brother. Even my beloved grandmother came from out of town to help care for him, instead of caring for me exclusively, as she'd done since I was born.

One day, shortly after he arrived home, I was sent outside to play, while everyone else stayed inside and rallied around Marshall. I fell on a sharp metal corner of a drainpipe, sliced open my right knee, and was rushed to the hospital for many stitches. Since then, I carry a large scar across my knee.

Lazaris takes hold of my right foot, and they shoot powerful energy, like a strong wind, through the sole, up my body, out the top of my head. This time, I feel overwhelmed with rage, jealousy, envy and feelings of being left out.

They are picked up and carried by the wind through my body and out the top of my head, quickly and thoroughly.

All is quiet. I wake up shortly after. All the pain in both my knees is completely gone! I mean gone! This was my first healing experience with Lazaris. I've had many more since then, but none as dramatic as this one.

I had no idea all that emotional crap was stored in my knees since I was two and a half years old. In hindsight, it was the only way I could express my rage and jealousy at being displaced and left out. It also put the attention back on me. It also set a pattern of putting my pain in my body.

Being fairly new to Lazaris and the work then, I just thought it was physical pain. This powerful healing taught and prepared me for deeper and more complex healings over the decades to come.

Learn more about Janis Rosen on page 4.

Walking My Path to Dignity

Yngo Gutmann

I was addicted to drugs. It all started when I was sixteen years old, when I smoked marijuana for the first time. I immediately loved it and wanted more. My life as a sixteen-year-old was wild and painful. I never tried to accomplish much at school, and my grades were accordingly bad. I didn't care, and I hated school. Instead, I made music, and I played the drums. I also painted and wrote poetry. I spent long days and nights with my artist and musician friends, all older than me.

But my life as a young person was pure chaos. I didn't feel held or cared for by the world around me, so I found myself wandering about, feeling completely lost. *This world is not for me*, I kept thinking. And, so, smoking that first joint was an absolute pleasure. Everything became easy. I laughed and had crazy ideas and insights. It was a couple of weeks before the next time my friends and I smoked marijuana. Finding the stuff wasn't easy in those days.

When I was nineteen years old, the Berlin Wall came down. The borders opened and what ensued was chaos that lasted for many years. I loved it because I didn't have to worry about what to do with my life. I was smoking every day by now. Smoking weed was no longer a luxury; it had become a habit.

I did, however, have other interests: I devoured esoteric books on bodywork, chakras, crystals and began attending seminars. There was always a spark in me that wanted more and felt drawn to these things.

Over the years, I had developed a cycle of using drugs for three months (by then, I was also taking LSD and other chemical drugs regularly), then being sober for the next three months, only for the cycle to start again. During the times when I was not using drugs, I felt strong and clear. Then, drugs again. Back and forth. I was depressed and hopeless. Whenever I started to build something for myself in my sober moments— a relationship, an idea, a project—I destroyed it again after three months.

I became a father in 1996. I was happy and hoped that I would make it this time, that my children would be reason enough for me to live without drugs. Unfortunately, that didn't work either. I was a seeker who couldn't seem to focus on his search. In 1998, I had another child, a son. I was so willing, trying so hard to get everything right. But, I was on the run, running from my addiction. But, there was no goal, nowhere to go.

One day, in the fall of 1998, I went to my favorite bookstore. I knew the owner well; I had bought countless books over the years. Mr. Berg took me aside that day, excitedly showing me two books. As soon as I saw them, their covers, something happened to me. I opened one of them, and there it was, that feeling I had been looking for since I could remember. These were the books *The Crystal Cities of Lemuria*[1] and *Lemuria, Land of Golden Light*[2], by Dietrich von Oppeln. I had money only to buy one of them, so I purchased *The Crystal Cities of Lemuria*. I finished it in one sitting. When I did, everything was ringing inside me, and I wanted more.

During the summer of 1999, I attended my first seminar with Dietrich von Oppeln. I smoked marijuana again afterward, but I hoped and thought that I would soon be able to get rid of it.

With Dietrich, I learned about character; I was introduced to the Goddess and finally got to know my life's purpose. I had waited so long for this. I had already attended a few seminars, but in none of them did I find the truth about the Goddess I had unknowingly longed for.

After meeting Dietrich, everything happened fast. In late 1999, I flew to the Millennium Seminar[3] in Orlando with Dietrich and other friends. It was there that I met Lazaris for the first time. It was a miracle that made me new. At the time, I didn't understand a single word of English, but I didn't care, because I felt the energy, and I felt the rightness of being there. Completely new paths opened up before me.

Back in Germany, it was a very bright January. I started smoking marijuana again in late February. I felt worse than ever. I felt guilty about myself and Dietrich and about my spiritual friends. It was unbearable. Dietrich knew about the drugs, but he never punished or judged me. On the contrary, he loved me and offered support.

But I couldn't bear it, because everything I had built for myself, all the fine, delicate new paths, were gone. And, so, I decided to cut ties with all my friends because they were all drug users as well. Now I was alone with myself and my addiction. The friends were gone; the addiction was not. I had no more support for trying to quit, and so I hid my addiction from most people. I started living a double life.

Nevertheless, I eagerly continued to attend Dietrich's seminars. I also worked with Lazaris here and there. But there was so much shame. Even though Lazaris said he loved me, I couldn't accept it. And, so, my double life's gap became wider and wider.

In August of 2016, I was in a very dark place. I was taking speed every day and smoking pot like a world champion. One day, I was sitting in a café. And there she was. "Can I sit here?" Marlene appeared out of nowhere. I was excited—her energy.

I felt something very strange, something new and familiar at the same time. After a long conversation, I went home and felt like I had been kissed by the wind. Two weeks passed. I really wanted to see her again. But we hadn't exchanged phone numbers.

So, I went back to the café every day. I followed my intuition. And there she was again. From then on, we met often. I immediately stopped using all drugs. All I cared about was that I was clear in my head, to be able to meet her. Our encounters were wonderful and intense. We talked about absolutely everything. Also about the drugs. We built a relationship of trust, and we laughed so much together. I had never had that before. I was sober for many months, longer than I had ever been before.

Even though I was more certain of my sobriety than I had ever been before, I ended up slipping back into my three-month on-and-off cycle after being with Marlene for six months. I could hardly believe it, yet what choice did I have but to live with it? The times I was sober were so beautiful and so creative. We did a lot of Lazaris blendings and meditations together, and there was so much light. I did things that I had always wanted to but never did. I felt new hope inside of me. I even thought about having another child with Marlene. But there was still my addiction. I tried so many things, and I believed that I would soon make it. I worked on my visions for my life. I really became a new person in those four years, all while going back and forth in my addiction. And then, the worst thing I could have imagined happened: I smoked again, and Marlene broke up with me.

That was in September of 2020. I couldn't believe it was really happening. I had played my game, bet it all, and lost. I fell deeper than ever. I kept thinking that the relationship with Marlene should have been my masterpiece. It should have been a triumph. Suddenly, I was all alone, again. I wondered if I could go on living at all. There was no future to look forward to. The day we broke up, I made the decision to never use drugs again. Sure, I'd made this decision many times before, but this time, something was different. I'd been preparing for this moment of choosing for a long time, for many years. I knew that, one day, I would be ready.

A few days after our breakup, I asked Marlene to join me for a ritual. A separation ritual, separation from Marlene, but, more importantly, separation from my addictions. I felt broken, flooded with pain; it was a new kind of rock bottom. It was also a mystical moment; there was a glow, a spark of love and hope. I felt that I only had two paths to choose from: I could either choose a new kind of life, or I could die. I also felt I wasn't ready to die, so I surrendered to this new path completely. I am forty-nine years old, and my soul calls me to new shores. It is difficult for me to accept that I lost my relationship with Marlene in the process, but that is where my path has brought me. I cannot understand everything that is happening, but I feel a rightness in the way things are unfolding. Everything makes sense from a higher point of view.

Because of my decision to open myself, I have been experiencing miracles after miracles. I've found healing in layers of myself deeper than I've ever known. I now have relationships with people I never allowed myself to have before, because I now have a drug-free future. The way I approach life has changed; all of a sudden, things can be planned, I can get involved and be more responsible. My creativity is bubbling and cooking. My relationship with my soul is more alive than it has ever been. I feel more and more depth. I continue to open myself to my spirituality in ways I never have before. There is a purity in me, one I have longed for all my life and never had, and that truly is a triumph. My meditations with Lazaris have taken on a whole new dimension. I hear so much of it as if for the first time. I have even allowed myself to meet my fairie friend and his family, and my magical tools are more present in my reality. I show up with openness and vulnerability. Most importantly, I am sober, which allows me to deepen the intimacy I have with myself.

In the last months, I've been able to heal a lot of pain. I do not understand everything. It feels like a mystery. But, I have found a certain sense of peace, also in not being with Marlene anymore. We are on good terms and are taking steps to build a true friendship. I often think she came into my life to show me love and light. Sometimes I feel a deep whisper, an agreement of both our souls to have come together to experience these very events. Oftentimes, it still hurts, but I am finding acceptance.

Now I even feel gratitude, real and true gratitude. I've taken meaningful steps and am so very happy about that. I still have to actively choose this new path every day, sometimes many times a day. But it is so worth it. Lazaris accompanies me; he is with me every day. His unconditional love helps me to accept myself again and again, to love myself again and again. Every day, letting more love in.

Yngo Gutmann lives in Leipzig, Germany. During the third moon landing, on February 5, 1971, he landed on Earth with his twin sister. His musical career began at the age of thirteen. He played drums in various bands. In May 2000, he founded his own drum school and is fully active as a musician. He leads "TeamDrums" with companies. Here, he drummed up with hundreds of people. Yngo is the father of three children.

Endnotes:

[1]von Oppeln, Dietrich, "The Crystal Cities of Lemuria," Book, Ch.Falk-Publishing, 1998.

[2]von Oppeln, Dietrich, "Lemuria, das Land des goldenen Lichts," Book, Ch.Falk-Publishing, 1997.

[3]Lazaris/Pursel, Jach, "Millennium Celebration with Lazaris" Concept: Synergy, 2000, Audio Recording.

Seek and Ye Shall Find

CeliaSue Hecht

In my twenties, I searched for my lifetime career and a place to belong. I wanted to become a writer but did not know how to get published. I left my home in New York and moved to Los Angeles at the age of nineteen.

In 1975, I met Rannette Daniels (Nicholas) through a cosmic joke. I had quit my office job declaring that I would never again work as a secretary. I also wanted to join a radical feminist therapy group. At the LA Woman's Building, a woman writer gave me a phone number. I called and was invited to an open house party in West Hollywood. It was not what I expected. But I stayed for hours after meeting this incredible woman who was very different from anyone I had ever met.

Rannette had a melodic laugh, a glow and light about her and an ironic sense of humor.

Later, I needed a job and sought Rannette's guidance. She wanted me to sign up for a weekly Woman's course. I did not know how I could due to my finances. She said that if I assisted her for ten days (without pay) she guaranteed at the end I would have a job. I balked but eventually agreed.

During the ten days, she led her first weekend Successful Living workshop and my job was to monitor the tape recorder in the back of the room. She led participants through a variety of communication exercises for two days, which were fun, challenging and valuable. I observed people from the back of the room. One man came into the workshop looking like a bulldog, very angry. At the end, his face had softened and he looked like a newborn.

I knew that working with this woman was what I had been searching for and at the end of the ten days, Rannette offered me a job as her secretary. This was unlike any job that I had ever had and soon I was leading workshops and seminars including a five-day interactive and transformational SLS experience seminar. I led seminars in LA and Munich, Germany with Earthplay. I also became a published writer and had many spiritual experiences. Rannette supported me to go for my dreams, many that had seemed unattainable before I met her.

In the 1980s, life changed and I moved to Florida to be with my family. I had already lived more of my life dreams than I'd ever dreamed were possible. I decided to complete my college education and received my BA in Communications. During my senior year, I reconnected with Rannette and her husband

Dafydd. They founded OIM (Obedience Intercessory Ministry), an international, interfaith, interdenominational prayer ministry. For three years, after my father's death in 1987, I traveled around the world with OIM praying for others and experienced many miracles. We visited many churches, synagogues and other religious venues. I explored Bangladesh, England, France, Germany, Greece, Holland, India, Israel, Singapore and Thailand.

Rannette was always searching and discovering new spiritual realities. During various meetings, she played tapes of Lazaris. Listening to Lazaris seemed odd to me. I could not understand the words and the accent. We were praying at churches. Some Christian church leaders preached against New Age teachings. We kept our Lazaris tapes a secret due to concerns about the reaction of others.

I was in India for eight months and listened to tapes trying to discern the wisdom. Still, I was skeptical. Eventually, back in Los Angeles, I went to my first Lazaris event. I was nervous and did not know what to expect. I walked into the hotel room with my heart fluttering madly. I had not talked with Rannette or anyone else I knew about being there. I was on my own (or so I thought) in this exploration.

That first night, I kept looking at Jach Pursel (Lazaris' channel) and wondering what was going on. Still, I persevered and continued going to events. I began to love listening to Lazaris speak. He had a way of talking with such candor and humor even broaching difficult subjects with humor. I attended many workshops in LA and SF and enjoyed the camaraderie of my fellow magicians. I anticipated my moment with Lazaris at the end of each weekend workshop when I would receive a few words and a special crystal chosen especially for me.

When it was my turn, I felt very loved. The way Lazaris greeted me was as an old friend. As an Enneagram Type 4 this was the ultimate gift for me. A blissful peak experience. The personal messages and kind gestures touched my heart. I floated on Cloud Nine for days afterward.

During lunch breaks, Lazaris friends shared and compared notes about the event. Ironically, it seemed as though each person was attending their own unique workshop. Everyone felt loved and special.

At coaching sessions with Rannette, she would recommend specific Lazaris tapes for me to listen to. Sometimes she would play a few minutes of a tape in order for me to hear pertinent passages that applied to me.

I also was led to resources such as Dr. Helen Palmer's book about the Enneagram Personality Types[1]. I cried my way through the chapter on Type #4. The first time that I heard Lazaris talk about the Enneagram Personality Types[2] I was shown that I was #1. Rannette played the Dr. Helen Palmer's Enneagram Personality Type Four tape at a coaching session and laughed about the accuracy of it.

She assisted me in evolving and reaching for my high side, #1. (Enneagram Personality is an ancient system with nine personality types. There is a bottom line for each personality type. For #4s it is feeling special, and we search for True Love, something we had but lost.). For #1's the bottom line is being right and perfect. The high side for #4 is the same for #1, it is to Create Something Special, going above and beyond themselves and their search for #4 True Love or #1 Perfection, the mission is to *be* the *light* of *love* in the world. There were also challenging times and magical results. Maybe I wanted to attend an event, but did not know how I could go, and the stars would align and I was able to go. During guided visualizations and meditations, I connected with my Higher Self and Unseen Friends and learned and healed so much.

At a weekend event, one Saturday night, Lazaris offered everyone the opportunity for a healing of our choice during the meditation. Before this event, I had sprained my ankle. I was walking around feeling sorry for myself and wearing an ACE bandage on my foot. During the meditation, Lazaris offered the healing and I refused. I realized that I had been receiving benefits from the injury. Attention and poor me, pitiful glances and assurances from others. A few days went by and one day, I said to myself, "Okay, enough is enough. I am done." I meditated and got to call my dance school. I asked them where the dancers went when they had sprains and strains.

They recommended a chiropractor and I went to see him. He unwrapped the bandage, turned me upside down on a zero-gravity platform and massaged my ankle. It hurt a lot and when he was done he told me to walk for twenty minutes. When I came back to his office, the pain in my ankle was gone and never returned.

Utilizing the ritual calling upon all of the elements from the *Releasing Your Dreams and Visions into the World* tape[3], I cast my dreams of living by the beach upon the wind-air, water, earth and fire. A year or two later, at a pool during a break at a Lazaris event, I met another participant who told me he had lived in a home near the beach in Bodega Bay. It sounded divine. We chatted and he told me that a woman friend of his needed someone to house/pet sit every year when she would be gone. He called his friend to see if she needed someone and voilà, she did. As I drove up the coast by the beach, I remembered that years before I had cast this dream upon the elements. Filled with gratitude and wonder, I enjoyed my new abode for a year. There was sunshine, rainbows and deer galore too.

At an Orlando, Florida workshop at the end of one of the meditations, people told me that Lazaris had called my name out loud. I had always wanted that but it had never happened before. I had not heard it and apparently, Lazaris spoke my name several times.

Lazaris often talks about listening to the whispers and when we don't, the messages keep getting louder until there are *shouts*. Years before my marriage, during an event, my Higher Self came to me in a very unusual way. I had always seen her as this ethereal spiritual being sort of like Glinda the Good Witch in the *Wizard of Oz*. But this time, she came to me dressed in a bridal gown, wearing combat boots and carrying a briefcase. It was absurd. I did not comprehend what she was warning me about. During a coaching session years later, I shared with Rannette about it and we laughed because it was totally representative of my marriage, a premonition from my Higher Self.

Lazaris also encourages and shows us how to heal our shame, pain, and trauma. He has said life was never meant to be so painful. And when you heal your own pain, there is less pain in the world.

Healing Shame and Pain

After being diagnosed with fibromyalgia, I was intuitively shown that it was time for me to heal my pain and shame. Dafydd Nicholas supported me in doing this, often sharing and recommending Lazaris Healing Pain and Ending Shame tapes,[4,5,6,7,8,9] and telling me about EMDR (Eye Movement Desensitization and Reprocessing) a trauma healing process created by Dr. Francine Shapiro. I learned about trauma expert, Dr. Peter Levine, author of *Waking the Tiger*.[10] And I took a one-year Healing Trauma (PTSD) course with therapist, Donna Hamilton, who had studied with Dr. Levine. All of this healing inspired by coaching with Rannette and Dafydd led to my being able to relieve 98% of my symptoms of fibromyalgia.

In recent years, I've mostly worked with the tapes I've downloaded online. Since Rannette passed away in 2015; my sweet dog of twelve years, Cici, went over the rainbow on September 12, 2019; and Dafydd passed June 14, 2021, I've struggled with my spiritual connections, at times feeling lost. Yet, whenever I connect with Lazaris via blendings and meditations, I feel uplifted, loved and inspired.

A while ago, I was feeling very low. I listened to the *"Time to Touch"* blending about Sirius.[10] I was yearning to connect with Star Beings and my loved ones on the other side. During this blending, I felt Rannette holding my hand, which was very soothing and comforting. In a recent dream, Rannette and I were laughing together. I've also had dreams with Cici and Cici has barked at me from over the rainbow.

There is a saying "Seek and ye shall find," from the Bible. I sought to find my life's work and a place to belong and that came true. Plus, I found my deepest wishes, dreams, fairy tales and magic, much more than I ever imagined, happened too.

CeliaSue Hecht loves to sing, eat chocolate, write poetry and screenplays and wear purple. She is bi-coastal, bipartisan, metaphysical, and communicates with humans, cats, dogs over the rainbow. Born and raised in NYC, she has lived in California most of her adult life. CeliaSue wrote four chapters in What Happened to the Hippies *and coauthored five romantic travel guides. Her 35+ years of professional research, writing and editing as a newspaper reporter, newspaper and newsletter editor, means you can read her work in* Vox Media, Reno Gazette Journal, Atlanta Journal Constitution, Las Vegas Review Journal, O, The Oprah Magazine, Parents *magazine and many others. Newsletters included* EarthSave, Head Start, Freedom Collaborative*, and she wrote Have Dog Blog Will Travel for thirteen years. CeliaSue traveled for three years around the world with an interfaith, international prayer ministry. She has delivered lectures, workshops and seminars on spirituality, relationships, money, health, and getting published to audiences all over the world. Now, she provides news from non-mainstream points of view at Laughter and Tears, celiasue.substack.com and more info about her can be found at: https://celiasuewords.wordpress.com/organic-writers-credentials/.*

Endnotes:

[1] Palmer, Helen, "The Enneagram: Understanding Yourself and the Others In Your Life," HarperSanFrancisco, 1991, Book.

[2] Lazaris/Pursel, Jach, "Harnessing Our Personality Drive: Lazaris Explores the Enneagram (Intensive Excerpts Only)," Concept: Synergy, 1998, Audio Recording.

[3] Lazaris/Pursel, Jach, "Releasing Your Dreams & Visions into the World," Concept: Synergy, 1991, Audio Recording, Discussion & Meditation.

[4] Lazaris/Pursel, Jach, "A Lazaris Blending: Healing the Scars of Anger, Hurt and Pain (Blending from the May 17 Online Conference)," Concept: Synergy, Audio Recording, Blending Meditation.

[5] Lazaris/Pursel, Jach, "A Lazaris Blending: Transmuting Fear and Pain: Healing Ourselves and Our World ~ November 2017, The Year of Valuation,". Concept: Synergy, 2017, Audio Recording, Blending Meditation.

[6] Lazaris/Pursel, Jach, "Ending Shame, Part I (Infancy)," Concept: Synergy, Audio Recording, Discussion, Meditation.

[7] Lazaris/Pursel, Jach, "Ending Shame, Part II: Psychic Contracts of Pain," Concept: Synergy, Audio Recording, Discussion, Meditation.

[8] Lazaris/Pursel, Jach, "Ending Shame, Part III: Those Adolescent Years," Concept: Synergy, Audio Recording, Discussion, Meditation.

[9] Lazaris/Pursel, Jach, "Ending Shame, Part IV: Adult Shame," Concept: Synergy, Audio Recording, Discussion, Meditation.

[10] Levine, Peter A., "Waking the Tiger: Healing Trauma", North Atlantic Books, 1997.

[11] Lazaris/Pursel, Jach, "A Time to Touch: Receiving the Light and Healing of Sirius," Concept: Synergy, 2021 Audio Recording, Blending Meditation.

Dorian A Faerie/Human Encounter

Keith Michael Thompson

It has been almost two weeks since hurricane Dorian[1] unleashed her power upon the northern Bahamas and certain coastal areas of the United States. What she has wrought has been described in terms, in words, that push the human imagination into realms of being and experiencing that challenge acceptance, forgiveness, and hope.

For seven days this consciousness captured the world's attention, as the elements reshaped land, lives, and the future, from Abaco to the Carolinas. Dorian brought fear and terror. Dorian brought despair, frustration, anger, and blame. Dorian in essence, brought the opportunity to face the deepest vulnerabilities that lie within the veils of the subconscious and unconscious minds. Yet, where there is darkness, light will eventually define the boundaries, and something different emerges.

Something new. Something more.

Many ask, and rightly so, "Why? Why has this happened? What is the value in experiencing such carnage and, in witnessing it?" This level of ambiguity may be a clue to a new story of hope. Wrapped in the energy of this questioning lies the resonance of mystery. Mystery that can be a guide to a myriad of answers that are as unique as each individual who has been touched by Dorian's kiss. Mystery more consciously embraced can lead to hope, seminal creative hope. The hope that births imagination that is wild, unencumbered, yet so delicately and solidly focused.

Dorian, in her brutality, was meticulous in her destruction. This meticulousness was on display in how she chose to move, defying the experts' imaginations in what she would do. Why does a storm grow when encountering land? Why does a storm maintain its strength and continue to unleash devastation upon an area and a people who just happen to be in the wrong place at the wrong time? Again, within the darkness of these questions, light can and will emerge. Maybe it is a light that guides one deeper into their self-doubt, revealing new strength and new talent that can illuminate a doorway to a new future. Or maybe it's the gift of understanding. Understanding a new relationship with the elemental world allows for new ways of living with the physical world.

The elements are speaking with humanity about change. When embraced, change can lead to a new harmony of living with the Earth, who is now growing in her own way. She is awakening to a new dream and a new potential that has never been. That level of resonance is now available to humanity. A resonance that will spark beauty. Beauty that leads to healing. This resonance can lead to new knowledge. A knowing that sparks courage and empathy that will change lives and the world. With these questions and new levels of knowing, I begin a journey with Faerie to work a magic of healing that can help all those wounded by Dorian.

I find myself in my safe place at the twilight of a day now ending. The moon is near full and fills my space with the love of the Goddess. The light is so gentle, so welcoming and embracing. I can hear the call of the Goddess to come now and love in a new way. My favorite grandfather oak shimmers in her light, and it is that light that captures my attention to come to sit there among the roots. Roots that run deeper than I know into the Earth, anchoring commitment and embracing water and its gift of love. His branches reach higher than I can see, embracing air and the gift of compassion and gently touching the light of fire and the passion it offers. Committed to loving with passion and compassion, I open myself to mystery and close my eyes, falling into a magical slumber.

I awaken in Faerie. Timoreia, Baa So Eea, and Salathe smile gently at me as I gather my awareness of where I am. Timoreia says, "It is time. Time to gather the wisdom of water and fire and in their gifts of love and the passion, that love can create a space for healing." I remember this place I'm in. It is a grotto whose walls are made of pure crystal. They are clear and luminous and reach up some forty feet high. I see a set of stairs lead to a pool at the bottom of the grotto. This pool is clear, tranquil, and I can sense a warmth emanating from it. Timoreia leads the way down the stairs and Salathe, Baa So Eea, and I follow. As we descend, Timoreia and Salathe begin to sing and clap gently. Baa So Eea begins to stamp his feet in cadence to the singing and clapping. Their primal music is absorbed by the crystalline walls of this sacred grotto. With each verse, the walls gently pulse and release light into the space. The light gathers into a multicolored ball over the pool, descends into the pool, and the water gently parts, revealing a doorway. We each pass through.

It is night as we enter this new space. The moon is high, and the light softens the shapes that surround us. I pause briefly to orient myself. Timoreia gently touches my shoulder, and in my head, I hear her say, "See not with your eyes, see with your third and fourth chakras." Somehow, I know exactly what she means and re-orient myself to see in that way. What I see shifts, and what was hidden in the darkness now jumps into definition. It is incredible. Now I'm sensing with my physical senses through the portals of my third and fourth chakras. I'm seeing, tasting, hearing, etc., through love and all vulnerability and honesty of my emotions. The space comes alive with information that wasn't there before the shift. I realize this new way of sensing allows this space to be different. I am different. My connection to my faerie family deepens. I'm engaging them with my vulnerability and my love. We each are different, but now we experience this space and place as one.

This is awesome! Enchantment hangs heavy in the space. The connection it creates is alive, deep, and rich. It is the glue, the foundation for the magic about to be worked. We now pause as one.

In this state of oneness, I settle. I become aware that I'm more powerful in this state because it allows a level of sensitivity in this wounded place. The moon's light is brighter now, and I can see that we have gathered near a dark pool. Throughout Abaco Island, there are these inland pools that define marsh and pine forest. The scars Dorian left are evident everywhere. The outline of broken trees is everywhere, and in the energy of this space, you can sense unease and an ache for harmony. The smell of death is heavy.

The four of us surround this tranquil pool. In the light, I can see other faerie magicians gather, as well as their human cohorts. I wonder why it is here that we have gathered. A faerie man speaks now. He and Baa Soo Eea are dear to each other. His energy is dynamic and fills the space with dignity and quiet courage. His words carry these emotional resonances as he begins to tell a tale of healing.

"The storm you call Dorian has illuminated many things in your world as well as ours," he begins. "Most prominently at this time, there is pain. The pain of abandonment. The pain of loss. There is, too, the pain of change. Pain in your world acts as a boundary, as a way to experience living as human. It gives definition and purpose for many. But this level of pain, when held onto as a way life should be, also stops growth from being the elegant liberator from one form to a higher form. The consciousness Dorian has seeded your world, not only with pain, but also with the knowing to heal it more completely, more easily." As he speaks, the space around us shifts with a growing power of dignity and courage. It is thick, and you can almost touch it. Within this deepening dignity and courage, we gather closer to one another around the dark pool. Through the eyes of vulnerability, I can see that there are twenty of us, five humans, and fifteen faeries. We all sit now, encircling the dark pool with our various presences. Timoreia begins to sing, as does the dear friend of Baa Soo Eea. Her song is higher and his more low, in pitch and tone. Then they shift, his higher and hers lower. Back and forth they sing a dance of the feminine and masculine, seeking a balance of presence.

Each of us now begins to sing gently. I somehow know what to say and how to sing it. My song is a lullaby of forgiveness. It is ancient. I sense that I have tapped a knowing from experiences in Atlantis, a time of great power and beauty for me. Each of us adds a new song, and the space shifts and brightens. I begin to sense the presence of water and fire awakening in and around us. With each new song added, the presence of water and fire grows stronger, and this chorus, I realize, is creating a foundation of healing the pain here.

The dark pool begins to acknowledge this chorus of healing voices by answering each song with its own. The best way to describe it is that the undines start to dance. Waves of color, some I have never seen before, swirl in and above the dark water. The surface of the water pulses with this light, and it begins to penetrate the depth of the pool.

The air around us begins to dance, a dance of passion born of the salamander. The moon pulses, and quiet waves of warmth bathe the now growing sacred space, we twenty beings have co-created. Fire and water dance in and among us. As the elements find each other's dance, a sharing happens, and what were two dances now become one beautiful, magical waltz of love. I feel this in my heart, as do the others. As this new harmony emerges, each of us, as if cued, begins to quiet our voices until there is only silence. It is glorious. We each realize that silence is the think tank of the soul.

From the edges of the sacred space, figures begin to emerge. Some are human-like and cloaked, while others shimmer with exquisite light. I realize they are the souls of each of us here. Our souls find their place among the now-gathering magic. I feel a rush of love fill me. A love that is, in one moment, deeply personal and, in an instant, connected to something magnificently larger than me, connected to everything. Again, the space shifts, and the pool is now a cone of light, pulsing with the knowing of twenty souls' love for humanity. A portal opens within the light of the undines' and salamanders' dance, revealing massive crystal formations. The island of Abaco rests, I realize, upon massive crystal formations.

Mystery sparkles all around us and, in this new resonance, we each begin to sing our songs once more, but now each song carries the power and love of our souls. With each new verse, waves of energy descend into the portal, infusing the crystal formations with this co-creative magic of love and healing for humanity, for the world, for the Bahamas, for the islands of Abaco and Grand Bahama, and for each individual enmeshed in their experience of what Dorian offers as gifts.

The portal of light now begins to dim and finally closes, and there is only silence. Beautiful, lush, loud silence. The moon's light paints this sacred place, and I look around me, taking in each individual here through my senses, enhanced by vulnerability and love. I quietly weep in acknowledgment of the honor of being a part of this.

We gather ourselves and begin our journeys back to our worlds, knowing that something beautiful, something mysterious, and grand has elicited a change in a world of pain.

There are now options for change that were not there before this ritual of human/faerie love.

Learn more about Keith Michael Thompson on page 85.

Endnote:

[1]Dorian was the most powerful hurricane to ever strike the Bahamas, a Category 5 storm. It struck the Bahamas on September 1, 2019. The World Meteorological Organization names storms alternating between male and female names. Although the assigned name, Dorian, is a masculine name, the author experienced the energy of the storm as feminine.

Me a Powerful Mapmaking Magician... Are You Sirius!?!

Michaiel Patrick Bovenes

On a beautiful May morning in 1995, a little over a year after the vortex of the Goddess opened, I found myself driving up to Atlanta. What in the hell was I doing? I had decided to attend another workshop I could barely afford when my life was riddled with struggle.

I shouldn't go. I never was a powerful "anything," my entire life, let alone a Mapmaking Magician. C'mon, give me a break! I was an imposter among all the others and should turn around and spend the weekend doing something more productive. My immature ego ranted off-and-on until I drowned it out with rock music while singing "Magic Man" by the band Heart.

Fast forward...the silence expanded in my mind as the meditation music faded away. Lying on a conference room floor with 250 people all around me, my life was about to change forever. I heard a voice in my mind calling a very unique name. It felt familiar to me, but was so very different from my birth name, or any other name I've heard before. Suddenly, I could see the name flashing in my mind, and the voice repeated itself several times. It didn't sound like my Higher Self; it was a melodic and beautiful tone as it repeated this magical name held together by only eight common letters.

I knew this experience was uniquely mine and wasn't being guided by Lazaris. Was this another experience of my imagination, imagining itself? I tried to let go of it when my Higher Self appeared, repeating the name as if to acknowledge me. I was delighted and frightened at the same time.

I was in my own world, but wanted to be sure I'd remember this, so I mentally repeated this name a few times to let it sink in. Instantly, I started feeling lighter, like my entire body was lifting off the floor and expanding exponentially. I tried to move it but couldn't. My body had doubled, tripled, and quadrupled in size as it continued filling the room.

I faintly heard Lazaris counting us up as I laid there paralyzed while filling the entire ballroom with my energy. At one point, I was concerned that my face was going to press against the ceiling. Intellectually, I knew it wasn't my actual physical body, but it was so real. I had never felt my presence so tangibly and with such energy. I became the space in the room. I could feel others as they were slowly stretching, coughing, and coming back from meditation.

I laid there motionless as Lazaris played a song to conclude the day. Thank God, because I still couldn't move. I repeated the mystical name once more and felt its magical resonance, and knew it was sacred.

The song ended, and I sensed the ballroom lights were full-on behind my closed lids. I remained completely still, in total ecstasy, confounded by my gigantic presence that was so light, yet my eyelids too heavy to lift. I didn't want this feeling to end. I felt powerful in a way I had never felt before.

A concerned fellow magician leaned down and whispered in my ear, "Are you okay?" Their words broke the spell, and I finally grounded myself enough to smile and nod my head slowly. My vision was blurred as I peered out into a half-empty room. I was glad nobody attempted to have a conversation with me as I gathered my belongings to leave; I was still somewhere else.

I always lodged at a more affordable hotel within walking distance from the seminar. As I walked out of the Hilton lobby into a warm May evening, night-blooming jasmine swirled through all my senses. It helped me to shake off the momentary confusion as to which direction I should turn to get to my hotel.

Twilight had ended as I walked down the sidewalk in a daze. Suddenly, it was very dark. I thought, *Oh, no, what's next?* Then I realized the streetlight above me had turned off. I was relieved to have a logical explanation for the sudden darkness.

It was a relatively quiet night for a busy street near one of the country's largest airports. As I approached the next streetlight, darkness fell upon me once again. I looked up, and the light was off. I turned my head back and noticed the previous streetlight was illuminated again. Hmmm...could my energy field be influencing the light sensors? *Naw*, I thought, *just a coincidence.*

Discarding the idea, I continued walking until I crossed the street toward my hotel. As I stepped up on the curb, it happened again. A third streetlight in a row shut down as soon I passed underneath it. I stopped in my tracks and felt a chill run up my spine as tears rolled down my face.

Something major had shifted within me. The seminar was *Igniting the Fire: Activating Your Passion for Life.* I had no words to begin to describe it. Nothing like this had ever happened before during these events. I was delighted and confused. I don't remember any more details from that night except that I was exuberant and exhausted.

When I got back home to Florida, I was hesitantly pondering if I should email Jach about my baffling experience during the workshop. I did. I didn't know who else I could share this with, who may have some inkling of what had happened.

Surprisingly, he responded the next day. He mentioned that I must be temporal lobe sensitive regarding the streetlights, and the eight-letter name I received was most likely my "magical name." It was to be held sacred and not shared with anyone, not even him. Jach also suggested that I invoke this name when I worked my magic to help align myself with this magical presence.

Out of curiosity, I googled the eight-letter name, and nothing appeared of any significance. Still, to this day, twenty-something years later, I've never heard it before, except when I mentally repeat it to myself. I will always keep it sacred. I've never felt the same expansion as I did that weekend, but I always feel a shift and lift of my energy when invoked. I guess the first time is always special like most things in life.

About six months later, Jach had posted about Cheiron numerology on the online forum. He shared a mystical numerology secret and why his spelling was slightly different from the common name Jack. He said, if your name's numerology matches the number of the day you were born, it can help align your resonance with your destiny.

Interesting, I was born on the 5th of December. So, five is my physical number. I added up my birth name, Michael, and it came to a four vibration. *Hmmm...bummer*, I thought. I played with different letters, and, if I added an "i" to Michael, it would be a match with my birthday.

I was eager to fulfill my destiny since I had chosen this to be my last physical incarnation and seriously considered changing it legally. Yet, a part of me was filled with self-doubt, and my ego's commonly felt hesitation.

That Friday morning, I was on my way to Asheville, NC, to speak at a Unity church service that Sunday morning. I would be staying at the minister's home while they were on vacation. I loved long drives; it was a time for me to reflect, think, and be with myself in solitude. This was way before iPhones became a permanent distraction in our lives.

I was still on the fence about changing the spelling of my first name. Halfway to Asheville, I connected with my Higher Self as I drove along I-95. I remember that I mentioned to him that I was thinking of changing the spelling of my name to Michaiel. I asked for a sign to confirm if this would help align me with my empowered destiny. We communed for a while, and I let it go, knowing I'd often receive a whisper in a day or so.

The sun was setting on Asheville's foothills, as I pulled into the driveway of the minister's home. As the dust settled from the dirt driveway, I found the hidden key and slowly dragged my overnight bag into the house. I was tired from the long drive and decided not to explore Asheville but to relax that evening, instead.

A welcome letter suggested I stay in the den where a sofa bed had been prepared for me. The den was beautiful, with lots of wood paneling, a large comfy bed, a window with a panoramic view of the mountains and hundreds of books surrounding me on the custom-made pine shelves.

As I unpacked my suitcase, I happened to glance up at the bookshelf above the bed, and a book immediately grabbed my attention. The title was, *Magick, Mysticism...*, and "something or other." It was an old book, and my curiosity caused me to reach for it. The first page I opened it up to, the name, "MICHAIEL," was staring back at me, before my very eyes!

I almost dropped the book. I realized my Higher Self had just confirmed my request from earlier that day. The chapter was referencing the ancient spelling of Archangel Michaiel, but I had never seen it spelled that way. I always saw it spelled Archangel Michael. I changed my name to this new spelling when I returned to Florida the following week.

Along with my experience in Atlanta, these powerful, magical, and life-changing events helped me embrace that I am a Divine Being from Sirius, a powerful Mapmaking Magician. Even though my ego used to roll my eyes when Lazaris suggested this to us, now I knew for sure.

My magical life continues to astound me, every day. I'll never take it for granted. I am still in awe as I picked just one book off the shelf of hundreds and opened it to the exact page with my new name on it. Even that would be impossible to be a coincidence. A miracle, yes. A coincidence…no! Thanks to all of my unseen friends.

I'm glad I didn't listen to my ego, who wanted me to remain small, hidden, and powerless on that May morning driving up to the workshop in Atlanta. I decided to keep the flyer and found it with the many things I treasure.

Lazaris quote on the flyer, *Igniting the Fire: Activating Your Passion for Life*:

> "Chiseled and carved lovingly by your Soul, cured and fired enthusiastically by your Spirit, your Passion for Life is a masterful artistry waiting to be unveiled. It waits to be activated — to be lived fully and richly. Come, ignite the fire. Marvel. Be amazed by what is revealed in the light." - Lazaris

Michaiel Patrick Bovenes is the new thought leader and founder of Soulutions for Moving Beyond Struggle. He is a gifted inspirational speaker-teacher and author of Developing Personal Peace. *His popular guided meditations are all rated 4.7 stars on InsightTimer. His main focus is on helping clients and students overcome resistance to change. In his own words, "My purpose isn't to teach anything new or tell you what to do. I'm here to help you remember and align with the truth of who you really are—a powerful spiritual being!" Michaiel's life-changing online video courses help people get unstuck and create positive change. Additionally, Michaiel is a life coach helping clients create the change they desire by aligning with their Soul's purpose, inner strength, wisdom, and empowered destiny.*

Walking a Labyrinth

Mary Woodhouse

We arrive using a GPS device for the first time. It was a challenge to abandon relying upon a paper map and to trust an electronic voice instead, but we made it. It feels good to be deepening our friendship by taking this adventure together. Jude and I have known each other for a few years. This trip is our second jaunt to find a labyrinth to walk. Our first attempt to walk a labyrinth failed. There was supposed to be one in a churchyard near where we often meet for tea. We looked and looked in the churchyard. We identified vague vestiges of a pattern, but the grass was so overgrown it was impossible to follow a path. Undaunted by this setback, we simply went to our usual spot to sip tea and talk for a while. We then used the Worldwide Labyrinth Locator[1] to find another possibility for another day.

Today is the day. This adventure is risky. We drove a long way to this unfamiliar rural location. What if this labyrinth is also overgrown and unwalkable? We are now on the beautiful grounds of The Healing Co-op, an organization that supports women who have cancer or are survivors. We see a large group of women meeting here for an early morning bike ride. Cars loaded with bikes on racks pack the small parking lot. We look around and don't see a labyrinth. We don't see anything that looks like the picture we saw on the internet. Uh-oh.

We ask one of the women where the labyrinth is. She points over to a field with small bushes. Then we recognize it. It seems the picture on the Labyrinth Locator website must have been taken years ago, when the labyrinth was newly built. The photograph was taken from above, and showed a simple design outlined in a field of grass. Now, eight years later, there are embellishments. Many short yew bushes, about two feet high, outline the path. Two blue hydrangeas stand on either side of the entrance. The entrance way is a columbine-covered trellis, full of purple blooms. In the center of the labyrinth are two stone benches.

Jude asks me how this works.

"Just think of a question that you want answered, then enter," I tell her.

"Should one of us walk the whole labyrinth, then the other?"

"No," I say. "It's fine to have more than one person in the labyrinth at once. You need enough time between each person,

so you don't crowd each other. It would take far too long to
have only one person complete the labyrinth at a time."

I have done this only once before; therefore, I am the
expert.

Jude takes a moment to think of what it is she would like an
answer for and enters. After giving her some time to walk
ahead, I prepare to enter.

Standing before the entrance, I asked for help with many
things. Help for my grieving process and how to help my
family grieve the loss of my sister to suicide six months ago.
Guidance for finding purposeful work. I also ask for direction
for developing my creativity. I don't have one question I need
an answer for. All these issues swirl in my head and weigh on
my heart. I wonder, can I receive answers to more than one
issue? Will this work? Am I sabotaging my results by asking for
too many answers?

This early June morning is overcast and warm. A mist hangs
in the air, blanketing the meadow, floating between the bushes
and trees. We are surrounded by the lush greenery of New
England fields and woods. As I take a step to enter through the
trellis, I notice the path is wide. I feel a sense of relief. The last
time I walked a labyrinth on Block Island, the path was so
narrow I felt I might fall over, as if falling off a balance beam.
Although this new path is wide, I still have to watch my step.
Ahead of me are little spiderwebs in the grass, everywhere! I
have never seen such a thing before. Every few feet, a small
beautiful spiderweb is cradled in the grass. The webs are about
four inches in diameter, slung between and over blades of
grass. Now, how, during a sacred walk, could I step on and
destroy such a beautiful little thing? At home, I often destroy

spiderwebs while cleaning the deck and patio. But now, it seems beyond inappropriate. As I look closer, I realize that I can only see the little webs because of dewdrops clinging like teardrops to each of the many threads. My heart fills as the insight flashes; my sadness, my tears, can make some beautiful things more visible. My grief can do that. If I allow myself to experience my grief, I can see things I've never seen before. Beautiful things, beautiful little things everywhere. And so, I must continue to walk carefully, consciously, in this labyrinth and in life.

Since Jude entered before me, and the grass is wet with dew, I see where her steps flattened the grass. Can I follow in Jude's footsteps to avoid destroying the little spider webs? This inspires the thought: can I follow in someone else's footsteps on my spiritual path? It could be one way of finding guidance and protection, yet we always want to experience our own path. I can't see all of Jude's steps clearly, but *sometimes*. Maybe *sometimes* walking in another's footsteps for a little while could be helpful.

As I walk, I continue to watch out—every step matters. So many webs to see and to step between. I think of the spiders' work and the metaphor of weaving, the beauty of the weaving. Each little web is a creative project. I, too, can have many little creative projects. I can weave my projects together rather than keeping them separate. I can be a weaver. This could lead me to purposeful work. With all the questions I stepped in with, the answers are coming, answers woven together, just as I can weave my creativity, my emotional healing, my finding purposeful work.

As I walk, I hear the voices of the women who are gathering here for their bike ride. Happy sounds wafting in the breeze. Many morning bird songs mixed with women's voices, laughing, greeting, planning, directing, exchanging information, gathering for an adventure. It's pretty cool to be doing this in a woman-focused location.

Jude reaches the two stone benches in the center. She sits on one of them. When I arrive, I take a seat on the other. We sit in silence, listen to the birds, look at the mist, contemplate until it feels time to walk back out. The benches face each other, but we are in our own space, not looking at each other at all. Jude starts on her journey out before I do.

As I follow the winding path out, a woman on a cell phone walks down to the edge. She stands near, but just outside, the labyrinth. The nerve! She moved away from her crowd for some privacy, and she is standing right next to the labyrinth during our sacred walk! Now I've got to overhear her loud cell phone conversation.

A rush of anger fills me. I tell myself to let it go, just stay focused. Eventually she moves, but she had been there quite a while, surprisingly long, surprisingly oblivious, totally annoying. Interesting to think there can always be, there will always be, some distraction, imperfections on the spiritual journey that bring up negative emotions to handle. I think of a friend who spoke of this once, noise in her house, opening a door, yelling "I'm trying to meditate in here!!" and the total contradiction in energy, of seeking peace and getting angry at the noise.

Continuing upon the path, I suddenly feel uncomfortable, confused. Have I been here before? Is the path out the same path as the path in? I don't remember this. I don't remember that. Where am I? How does this work? What is the path? I should know how the path works, like a map. I should have studied the map, and I should know what I am doing. What is the big picture? Here I am, watching every step, but I don't understand the big picture! I am distressed, almost panicked. But, then, I realize, there *is* a greater design. I may not know the details of how it works, but I am *held by the design*. I *will* make my way out just as sure as the sun will set tonight and rise again in the morning. In life, too, I am held by a greater design. There is a connection of the human body to the earth. This connection is fundamental to how the design works. We walk on the Earth, within a design created by the Divine. In a moment, I feel lifted, touched by the Divine. I feel some of my grief and guilt lifted out of me. As lost and confused as I was in trying to help my sister, as tragic, as sad, as heart-rending as her death was, there is a greater design in which we are all held in love, both she and I, all our family too. I feel it deep in my bones. My spirit is lifted, my heart is lifted, I am filled with wonder.

Nearing the end of the walk, but well before I step out, another rush of feeling. I had the same feeling in the labyrinth on Block Island last summer. This particular, unique, physical labyrinth I walk, here in a field in Middletown, RI, is connected to all other sacred labyrinths, through all space and all time. This labyrinth is an expression of the *One* labyrinth that somehow lives beyond space/time in the mind of God/Goddess/All That Is. A feeling that, when I stepped into this space, into the sacred labyrinth, I entered the *One*, the First One. I am walking within an *Idea*, expressed in the physical. A Sacred Idea that brings insight and healing. A gift from God/Goddess/All That Is. And today it has lifted me, brought me healing. It is a design, a relationship. It is a divine design, an activity that brings what you ask for. This is an exercise in Asking and Receiving, and in connecting to the Mysterious Divine.

Approaching the end of the labyrinth at the same trellis where I began, the hydrangeas on either side sport their big blue pom-pom blooms. Due to who knows what—soil, sun, drainage—one of these is much smaller than the other. Living things don't grow equally. They grow the way they grow. Even when you expect or desire equal development, two livings things won't grow the same, but both are still beautiful. My sister and I were different, but we are both beautiful in our own way.

Stepping out of the labyrinth, I am filled with wonder and gratitude for the insights, for the place, for my friend. Jude and I sit for a bit to share our experiences before we head home. This, too, is a gift.

How accessible, yet profound, this type of meditation is. Pay attention, walk. Ask and be open to receiving. That's all really. Anyone can do it. No GPS needed.

Learn more about Mary Woodhouse on page 101.

Endnote:
[1]https://labyrinthlocator.com/, launched 2004, The Labyrinth Society and Veriditas, Inc. with the Faith, Hope and Love Foundation.

.

A Magical Gift from Lazaris: Solitude

Kathy Tountas

Lazaris has gifted us with many magical tools. One that has had a powerful impact on my life is Solitude[1]. It is a beautiful technique with which you create a sacred space guarded by the four directions, and once there, you create, by your intention, a silence that holds you in its stillness. You do not move, or even think, but you sit and wait...open, as if an empty vessel, willing to receive. You hold this space for ten minutes, if possible, and if nothing happens by then, it won't, so you may feel free to leave. Lazaris gave us a quick ritual to enter and exit by feeling the four directions' energies. Instead of entering the traditional way, moving clockwise, you enter going counterclockwise and exit moving clockwise. I wondered about the purpose of entering this way and realized that we would be entering a space already created, as it existed in the more real. We would be backing into it instead of creating it ourselves. I find this a profound mystery.

Each time I entered Solitude, I used his instructions by moving through steps 1 through 4:

Step 1, to enter, I began in the East; I was conscious of breathing air in a circular breath.

Step 2, moving to the North, I felt grounded with my root chakra deep in the earth.

Step 3, moving to the West, I felt divine energy flow through my being as water flows.

Step 4, from the South, I felt the warmth of fire as caring and compassion for myself.

I performed these acts as closely as possible, feeling each energy. I did move slightly, but I managed to allow the thoughts that appeared to drift away. Nothing happened for three evenings. But, on the fourth, very soon after entering the sacred space that the ritual creates, my four-year-old granddaughter, Emma, came in. I felt Lazaris' presence in the background.

Emma smiled and said, "Hi, Grandma," and climbed into my lap. This was a few days after watching her in a singing telegram to her aunt in honor of her aunt's birthday. I watched it a few times, amazed at the maturity she displayed for someone so young. In that moment, I realized that I was sensing Emma's resonance energetically. We momentarily enjoyed each other's company and the love we felt for each other. I shared a special connection with this child. Shortly before her birth, I created a ceremony in meditation to include my Higher Self, the Higher Selves of my son and daughter-in-law, Lazaris, and other spiritual beings I wanted present to witness the promises I planned to make. Unexpectedly, the Higher Self of the unborn child appeared. (My son and daughter-in-law did not give away the name they chose for their baby, as a way to keep from being pressured by family members!) But Emma's Higher Self was delightfully happy, with a sweet and joyous presence. I introduced her to Lazaris, and she laughingly replied, "Oh, I know Lazaris!" Her energy seemed to fill the space with delight, movement and grace. And this little girl standing before me was already beginning to display those qualities.

I said, "Emma, I watched your singing telegram to your Aunt Julia. You have such a presence, self-confidence and grace."

Emma said, "You saw all that in me?"

"Oh, yes, you're like a flower beginning to open, and your perfume is beautiful! You give me much hope for the world you will inherit."

As Emma observed me, I felt the complete trust she had in me. She said, "Grandma, will you dream me a visionary for my world?"

Confused, I couldn't immediately respond. Lazaris had spoken often about our world's need for visionaries to dream other visionaries awake. At the time, I had been reaching out for an answer as to what exactly a visionary was. I felt severely limited by my inability to visualize. Admitting my inability to fulfill her request, I was honest and replied, "I don't know what a visionary is, sweetheart. I am searching for an answer, and as soon as I know what being a visionary means, I will dream you one."

Emma looked at me solemnly and said, "Would you like me to tell you?"

I quickly answered, "Yes!"

She leaned forward as if to whisper a secret in my ear. "A visionary is one who envisions the world as good, just and divinely inspired."

And as I dwelt in the words, which were more than words, I sensed a fuller energetic meaning surrounding them, a deeper and richer energy with deeper meaning. Hearing the word "just," I mentally recoiled a moment, thinking of it only as punitive. But as I opened to it, I realized it was a way for a soul to grow, to experience the consequences of its actions. And then I remembered Lazaris saying, "What goes around, comes around...if you let it." And around that time in my life, I became aware of something I had created that had negative consequences, and I didn't want to experience the pain and punishment of it, so I asked Lazaris to help me. He worked with me that night, and when I awoke, I realized I was free of the negative Karma. And I remembered all of this in a moment, and I said to Emma, "Well, I can do that now!"

So, as she stretched out in my lap, Goddess entered my body and said, "I envision you and declare you to be a visionary for your world, good, just and divinely inspired. So be it and so it is!" And with those words, Goddess proclaimed Emma also to be good, just and divinely inspired. And I knew she also received her concept of just, or justice, with the knowing that what goes around comes around...if you let it. I know that she received the benefit of my work.

Satisfied, Emma climbed down, smiled at me and said, "Goodbye, Grandma."

Amazed, I said to myself, "I thought I was not supposed to move or think in Solitude, only be open to receive." I felt Goddess smile, and she said, "We can dialogue," and Lazaris added, "You're finding your voice."

This interaction in meditation also had a wonderful impact on my relationship with Emma. Her mother's entire family—grandparents, aunts, uncles and cousins—took a yearly vacation together in Florida, and their next visit coincided with the timing of this meditation. I visited them at the resort where they stayed, enjoying the hectic activity created by the other children. And when it was time to leave, I said to everyone, while looking at Emma, "Well, I'll be going now." Emma's eyes filled with tears, and she shook her head "no." I sensed her pain, a mirror image of my own at leaving her. I went to her and held her in my arms. Her voice trembled with emotion, as she said, "When will I see you again?"

I was planning on moving from Florida and returning to Michigan to be close to my family. I answered, "This is February. I'm moving in April, so I'll be back with you in two months!" She nodded, having something to hold onto.

Lazaris told us that there were two ways to know someone, through pain or through love. This deeper knowing of my granddaughter, heart to heart, was knowing through pain, a pain caused by separation. It was tender and touched us both deeply. But I much prefer to know each other—more, to know all others—through love.

After returning to Michigan, Emma and I still enjoy a close and loving relationship.

She loved the many crystals and stones surrounding me when she visits, so I began to teach her about their energy and how to respect them. That progressed to my giving her one each time we were together. Emma has her own collection of crystals, as does her sister, and even her four-year-old little brother.

I cherish my relationships with my grandchildren as we grow to know each other with love. But the lesson Emma and I shared, learning how much we loved each other as we stood in our mutual pain, is one that created an indelible knowing, even a scar, created by separation from each other, separation from love.

Taking that lesson and using it as my motivation, my commitment, I leave the pain of not being loved to the past, as I welcome each day and the opportunities I find to love.

Learn more about Kathy Tountas on page 109.

Learn more about Kathy Tountas on page 109.

Endnote:

[1]Lazaris/Pursel, Jach, "The Magic of Solitude," Connecting with Lazaris Series, Concept: Synergy, August 1992, Audio Recording.

Lazaris and My Family

Janis Rosen

L azaris has touched many members of my family, from the cats to my father and brother. Here are some of those stories...

Poppy and Lazaris

Poppy, my cat, died when she was eighteen years old after a long, full and beautiful life. I loved and adored her, deeply and completely. She was my Familiar, my teacher and my joy. I'd be lying in bed in the morning, having just awakened, my eyes not yet open and hear a voice in my head, "Good morning!" I'd open my eyes and there was Poppy, walking into my room, tail held high. Poppy loved to come and meditate with me when I would put on a Lazaris recording.

She'd been ill for a long while and I was looking after her at home, but the day came when she got worse. That last afternoon, I drove with her to the veterinary hospital. When it became clear that it was time for her to go, I told her what a wonderful job she had done with her life, how much I loved her, and that, when she got to the other side, she should celebrate her wonderful life. I said goodbye and held her as she passed. I asked Lazaris to meet her on the other side and help her along.

I wrote in my journal that night: Poppy died today. Tuesday, July 10, 01, at just before 3 p.m. On the final ride with Poppy to the vet hospital, I turned on the radio. A song was playing, with the words, "I am going away to a place I cannot describe, I am going away and I'm here to say goodbye."

I came home without her, kind of in the shock of grief. I called my dear friends and told them she'd passed. They had been part of the process and my support. They said to come over for dinner, so I wouldn't have to be alone.

The drive over was a familiar route, taken many times over the years. I stopped at a red light on the corner of Stradbrooke Avenue and Osborne Street. In front of the fire hall on the east side of the street, stood a tall metal art structure, that held a series of bells that never rang. As I paused at the red light, the bells chimed the song, "Deck the halls with boughs of holly, fa la la la la la la la la."

It was summer and the bells played! The light turned green, and I continued on my way, knowing my Poppy was celebrating a remarkable life.

How My Dad met Lazaris

Every summer, my dad and I would do an eight-hour drive to visit my brother, who lived away. Dad was a sweet, old soul, a man fully at peace with his Jewish faith. His spirituality was such a natural part of him and woven deeply into fabric of his being.

The one driving got to choose the music. In those days, we listened to cassette tapes. When Dad drove, he chose Frank Sinatra, Barbra Streisand, Neil Diamond, Bette Midler, and various show tunes. We'd listen, sing along and talk about life in the comfortable, easy way we had with one another.

When my turn came, I'd get into the driver's seat, pop out Barbra, pop in Lazaris, and head on down the highway. I'd bring my current, favorite Lazaris cassette tape on the trip to listen to.

Dad would say the same thing every year upon hearing Lazaris' voice. "Who is *that?*"

"It's Lazaris, Dad."

"Oh. What is he, a psychiatrist?"

"No, he's into personal and spiritual growth."

Dad would listen for a few minutes and then fall asleep and let his unconscious take it in.

I loved those intimate hours of driving down the highway with Dad asleep by my side, listening to Lazaris. Even though Dad was mostly asleep when Lazaris was on, I felt like we were experiencing it together. He would wake up to the sound of their voice, listen for a few drowsy minutes, stretch, and say, "Want me to take over now?"

Bye-bye Lazaris, hello Frank Sinatra. No big deal. And on down the highway with me, Dad and Frank doing it his way.

On our last car trip together, when I put on Lazaris, Dad said, as usual, "Who's that?" Then, "Oh, it's Lazaahris!" And he smiled a soft smile. He stayed up and listened a little longer this time before drifting off to sleep.

Marshall's Wedding

After ten years of dating the same girl, traveling and working together all over the world, my brother, Marsh, is finally getting married. As Dad and I drive to Minneapolis for the wedding, the weather is bleak, with heavy clouds and rain pelting all through the Dakotas.

They've planned a weekend of outdoor activities, including getting married outdoors. There is a bad weather backup plan to bring the wedding indoors, at the venue, but the rest of the weekend is centered at their home on the lake, with boating, barbecuing on the deck and celebrating with many loved ones who have traveled from near and far for this wonderful celebration of marriage.

That evening when we arrive, my brother and I are standing by the living room door and watching the bleak weather report on television. He turns to me and asks if there is anything I can do about the weather. Now, if you knew my brother, a medical doctor and researcher, the request to work on the weather is out of character to say the least. I look at him to see if he's joking, but there is a look of true asking in his eyes. He and I have never talked spirituality, metaphysics or Lazaris, and, needless to say, it's a very strange, or possibly desperate, request. I say that I don't know, but I will try.

Upon going to sleep, I ask Lazaris for help with the weather. I haven't done any weather magic as yet and don't know how. That night I have a dream. I am in a rowboat with Lazaris on the lake. The water is calm and still. The night sky is clear, blanketed with stars. They talk with me for a long time. We talk about water and much more. Lazaris and I make magic together.

The next morning of the wedding, the sky is a gorgeous blue, the sun is shining, and the weather is beautiful. It stays that way throughout the weekend. The night before we leave, I happen to catch the weather report on television. The satellite photo shows the entire state covered in heavy clouds, and it's been raining non-stop all weekend. Except, there is a beautiful round circle of clear blue sky around Minneapolis. The next morning as we pack up the car to head home, the sky turns cloudy, and the rain starts to pelt. As I say goodbye to my brother, he hugs me and thanks me for the good weather, and we never speak of it again. In the years and decades to follow, he's called on me two other times to do healing and make magic together.

Learn more about Janis Rosen on page 4.

Cancer to Cured

Dana Cummins

"Well, you've got more pathogens in you than most dead people," said the acupuncturist. I secretly smiled. I loved being an enigma people couldn't figure out. I had consciously called death to me, and it manifested as cancer. I believed, if I chose to do so, I could heal it as well.

"It's a tumor on your bladder. I'll need to see you three times a week until we get a handle on it. It's funny. I just said to God the other day that I was ready for a tough case."

"I know," I said, "I've been waiting for a month for you."

My regular MD/NMD told me they didn't know why I was still alive. The lab had stopped counting when they'd reached 2 billion pathogens, beyond which I should have been dead from kidney failure. He wanted to do more tests because he didn't know what I may be dying from or why I was still alive. I told him, "Thank you, no." Not only did I have no insurance, I hadn't had much luck with Western medicine in my life. And, most importantly, my body—my soul—wanted a different approach.

I would have gone to see the doctor earlier, but my partner had come down with staph, so I shoved down the impending collapse I felt and took care of her. All the while, I continued with my work, so we'd have money for our bills. When I asked my guides, they told me to be patient. It would take a bit, but I would know when the person I was to work with would be available. So I waited, sick but dealing.

A month later, while hosting a Psychic Faire at the local Pride Center, a friend and psychic told me about a local acupuncturist and Chinese herbalist who was helping her husband. I knew the moment she spoke those words that this was for whom I had been waiting. I called the next day and scheduled an appointment.

Somehow, I managed to add more to my plate and fit in three visits a week for my healing. Each time I laid on the table, waiting as the needles did their thing, I would go deep into meditation and talk with my unseen friends. My higher self never left my side, always there to support and guide me, Lazaris, Jesus, God and Goddess, Quan Yin, my soul, and future self—to name a few of my beloveds that assisted me with my healing. It was the most time I had spent with them in a long time. Between being self-employed, having several contracts, caring for my partner and our house, and working with her in running the local Pride Center, I worked eighty hours a week with only one to three days off a month for, well, I can't even remember how long.

The hardest thing about it all is that I remember the day I called death to me. There I was, outside, sun shining brilliantly on my face, drying the tears as they streamed down my face. I had given up. It had been just over twelve years that I had been embracing life, and now I was willing to let it all go again.

The beginning of our relationship had been like a dream. We connected deeply on so many levels, remembering past lives together. We dreamed our lives out. Together, we were going to help make the world a happier, healthier, and safer place for all. Then one morning, we woke up, and I rolled over, but she was gone. The shell of her body remained, but all the connected adventure was gone without a trace. The person now inhabiting her body was a scared, angry, and manipulative shell of a person. Gullible and hopeful, believing that the person I fell in love with would surely return if I were just patient and loving enough, I stayed. It took me two years to understand the gaslighting, another to learn to stand up for myself, and another to fall into hopelessness. I continued in the torturous relationship for seven more years before it ended in a two-year battle of learning to stand up for myself. I learned a lot in this relationship and have done significant forgiveness work for allowing it to go on for so long.

It was hard to go to the clinic so often. Looking inside, listening to all the pain, and doing a bit of healing, finding and changing beliefs on every visit. I had been coming for eight or nine months. The tumor was not responding, and the acupuncturist was scared. She was afraid I was going to die on her table. She had been calling around to all the doctors she knew, hoping someone else would take me on. She was not able to deal with the thought of me dying on her table.

She came into the room where I lay, motionless with a dozen or so needles sticking out of me. "Well, I left a message with Dr. Sandbridge, and I think she might be willing to take you on," she stated.

"I'm not interested in seeing anyone else," I said. "I was told you were who I should work with."

"But I haven't helped you, Dana. You might die!"

"Fine, I'll get rid of my death urge then," I said.

"What? You have a death urge?" She gasped.

"Well, of course I do. I'm dying, aren't I?" I replied.

Later, as I was resting in a client's recliner where I was house sitting, I heard a sudden loud bang on the window. It was so loud, I jumped from the chair. I went out to the deck, looking for what could have made such a noise. Not seeing anything, I turned to go back inside. As I turned, I saw it: a bird had flown into the window and lay motionless on the deck. As I scooped up the little bird, her death touched me deeply. I carried her back inside with me. Sitting in the recliner, I held the bird in my hands and began to cry. Not a pretty cry, but a cry that sent the tears and snot flowing down my face. My heart burst open, and I must have released five years of torment and sadness. I struck a deal: let the bird live, and I'll release my death urge. A second later, the bird stirred in my hand. I jumped, clasping my hands around the bird so it didn't flop out of my hands. Oh, my! Had it just been stunned? Did it come back to life? Did my vow still count? These were all questions that flew through my mind in seconds.

Holding the bird to my chest, I walked briskly to the door and went outside. The day was chilly, high in the pine forest, the surroundings frozen and still as a picture. I found a place by a tree and laid the bird in a nest of leaves. I stood back, took a seat on the icy bench, and waited. Eventually, it came to, wobbled about, took a few steps, then flew up to the nearest branch.

I knew I had to keep my vow. Now to figure out how.

Laying in my bed, meditating, back in the habit again, I looked up as my bedroom door opened. A cloaked and hooded figure, scythe in hand, moved towards me. "*No!*" I screamed at the top of my lungs. "Get out of here! I demand it in the name..." Stopping mid-sentence, sensing I had been slapped, the signature of my higher self rang, yet impossible. My higher self had never been anything but loving, kind. Surely, that must be my ego. "Be still," I heard. Terrified, I felt frozen in the bed, laid out with the cloaked figure standing next to me. Time slowed. The cloaked one turned to "look" at me, though they had no face. I watched as they took the scythe and brought it down. More terrified, thinking they were killing me, I saw the scythe slice through the middle of me. They brought the scythe back up to their side, looked back at me again, turned, and in silence left the way they came in.

I was still alive! What?! I looked down while reaching out to my higher self. What I saw was my tumor, floating there, sliced off of its stem. It appeared that death had killed my cancer. I was scheduled for a session at the clinic later that afternoon. When I went in, the acupuncturist muscle tested me and was stunned. The tumor was now floating free. We went to work disintegrating it. She, with her acupuncture and Chinese herbs, both with our intentions on the needles and herbs as much as our visualization on the tumor-shrinking, being absorbed and released by my body. All in all, it took me nearly a year to come back to health, though it took many more years to let go of the relationship. With the willingness to release my death urge and my follow-through by choosing life, I allowed death to help remove the manifestation of my death urge.

Within months, my higher self guided me to open up the Co-Op so that I could live my dream, even if it meant doing it without my partner's involvement. Within weeks of receiving the message, a group of friends and clients opened the doors of Mountain Spirit Co-Op.

Being devoted to my spiritual life in a new, consuming way was what I had longed for all of my life. It was a dream come true. As I continued to grow and heal, the Co-Op grew and expanded into a well-known and loved gallery, healing center, yoga studio, lending library, and conference room. It brought me to life as I'd never felt before.

We were working with thousands of people from all over the world. Daily, people would come in "just to be in the energy." They would claim it was the only place in the world they had ever felt accepted for being themselves. At least ten people a day would give us this message. So affirming it was for us and our mission to hold space for all, to be supportive and compassionate. I loved holding people, hugging them with an open heart and depth that acknowledged and appreciated them on all levels. It often brought people to tears, even strangers.

They would say it was the first time that they ever felt seen and loved for just being themselves. I love that I can do that. It is one of my superpowers. And I want to share it with anyone who wants it. We all deserve to be loved, seen, and appreciated. I learned so much during the thirteen years the gallery and center held space downtown. Hundreds of practitioners joined us over the years, and though we ran the center as a Co-Op, I was the sole owner and was responsible for our integrity to be kept in the highest regard. That meant learning to communicate with dignity and compassion, something that I hadn't mastered by a long shot, and I allowed ample opportunities to practice and became better at it. So many skilled, talented, and gifted people joined us. It was a great honor to get to know them and witness their talents. I was surprised to meet so many talented and gifted people who were unwilling to allow success. Most, including myself, were never supported or even allowed to share their gifts and talents. So many had come from repressed backgrounds, all learning to heal the wounds of the past. We were known as "the trading Co-Op" for the first two years. And members continue to trade with each other to this day. Supporting each other in our healing and our growth is valuable and is a treasure for which we are all grateful.

The doors may have closed to the gallery and center, but we all continue our work. The Co-Op continues to advertise and support practitioners from around the country. We are Artists, Healers, Readers, Musicians, Teachers, Astrologers, and more. Anyone working in their integrity with dignity and respect for all people is welcome. We consider ourselves a phone book of "People Doing Good Work in Their Community" and hope to be global in 2022.

The Lazaris Material principles are what brought this into creation, creating a safe place of belonging. A place to grow and share, while being nurtured and respected. A place that honors and respects all walks of life, all religions, non-religions, races, genders, orientations, and preferences. A place to flourish and have fun co-creating with an incredible group of magicians. When Jach Pursel joined as a member, it was a dream come true—so confirming, I almost burst with joy. Lazaris has been with us every step of the way. From my healing to prompting me to open the doors. He has helped co-create each phase of the project, magically and lovingly, backing me with more love and compassion than I've ever known.

We are very blessed, and the founding core *of people* is still the founding core after fifteen years, which says a lot, if you ask me. We have all made huge strides in our personal growth, as well as in our love for each other. MSCO is our safe place to be supported and loved as we come together and create a synergy like none other. It has been my honor and my grace to hold space for something far more magical than I could have conjured on my own. It has given me more love and purpose and so much meaning in my life. It is my continual learning center, with so many outstanding teachers.

Learn more about Dana Cummins on page 55.

EPILOGUE

My Magician's Way

I wander among the forest trees aimlessly, lost and alone, wondering where I am, how will I know my way, will I ever feel connected…

A voice in the night speaks to me. We offer a Way, a path out of the darkness into the light of connectedness, out of the dark woods and into the gracious love of belonging.

I am astounded and hopeful. The Magician's Way, a path out of this eternal loneliness, a way forward. I am overcome with gratitude.

I look for my mound to begin and there it is. I stand in my vulnerabilities of strength and weakness, realizing the grounding nature of this acceptance.

I embrace my varied selves, my Higher Self and Soul, God/Goddess/All That Is, my ever-present orphan child and waif, my nurturer and warrior, my wise one … I am connecting.

I face the light of the East, feeling the balmy breeze
The South's fires warm and energize me
West's waters are nourishing and flowing
And the lands of the North are strong and powerful
I am in my elements

I stand tall on my mound, empowered, yet knowing there is more

I summon my unseen friends
My graceful Soul and precious Higher Self stand to either side of me, holding hands

God/Goddess/All That Is surround and embrace me
Lady Morgaine and my Trusted Knight are nearby along with
the Mysterious Stranger
Fairie Queens and Kings gather
And my Future Self shines
I feel loved and supported

I look for the portals
The light is enchanting, the air shimmers and charms
The clouds mingle and the birds beckon
Trees whisper in the breeze and the stones speak of dreams

I am ready to stand tall on my magician's mound and receive
my accoutrements
First my wayfarer's cape, emerald green, flowing and
magnificent
I feel it strong and protective on my shoulders, surrounding me
I receive my sword and sheath it on my left hip, my chalice
hangs from my right
The shield is sturdy in my left hand and my trusty staff secure
in my right

I am complete
Connected, empowered, supported
I have what I need
Life stretches before me and I can walk these paths in my
wholeness

What do I want?
The crucial step.
Here is the growth, the quivering awareness that I can choose
No longer lost and alone
I am loved, I belong, I can create

I choose love and connection, for myself, for all
I choose happiness and joy

I choose to learn and grow, giving and receiving my gifts

I choose my Magician's Way and I send my eternal love to my friend Lazaris, and all my Magician friends, seen and unseen.

I am whole.

Pamela Dickson

Pamela Dickson has practiced many spiritual and healing traditions over the years, including Western and Eastern medicine, Jungian psychology, Kabbalah, and, of course, Lazaris teachings. She enjoys writing poetry and short essays, wandering among the nature elements, and listening to the music of the stars.

ACKNOWLEDGEMENTS

Many people's support and efforts culminated in the publishing of this book. My wife's love and encouragement nourished me throughout this endeavor. Patricia Walkar and Pamela Dickson have been talented, dedicated volunteers over the past many months of story development and book building. They were my sounding boards and participated in far too many activities to list, including the book cover design. A special thank you to Patricia, for contributing her astounding artwork "Close to Home" to grace our cover.

Valerie Yersh helped to initiate the project, including guiding the authors' group in her beautiful *Future Weaving* meditation. Molly Gregory educated me on the basics of publishing and gave wise advice. Pauline Dolan participated in story development with authors and hosted various fun Zoom sessions. All our magician authors have been a joy to work with as they shared their writing, vulnerability, and enthusiasm.

Dana Cummins contributed her wholehearted cheerfulness and encouragement. She brought many new authors into the project, suggested the use of Grammarly, then assisted authors in using it. Erin Kampa and Patricia Walkar warmly assisted authors with that exercise as well. Michaiel Patrick Bovenes took us all on a lovely co-creation meditation near the final phases of the project.

We are deeply grateful to Jach Pursel for his early encouragement, for supporting us all by sharing his story and writing such a beautiful, powerful foreword.

We all very much appreciate Dietrich von Oppeln's sparkling, enthusiastic generosity of offering online access to his Music for Lazaris to readers who purchase our book. Pamela Dickson, Patricia Walkar and Keith Thompson made appreciated contributions toward project costs.

Dana Cummins, Tysa Goodrich, CeliaSue Hecht, Erin Kampa, Carole Sainte-Marie, and Patricia Walkar all helped with final proofreading. We also thank our professionals, Shannon Cave for copyediting, and Michelle Woodhouse for graphic layout and file creation for the book cover.

Again and always, gratitude for Jach Pursel, a great mystic, for being willing and able to be the Channel for Lazaris these many years. Thank you to everyone who has ever been involved with publishing and distributing the Lazaris Material™ through Concept: Synergy. And of course, we all feel boundless thanks to Lazaris, who brings love, information, techniques and so much more to our world, through Jach. This entire book is an expression of gratitude for Lazaris, who has provided humankind with an unmatched compilation of personal growth material to explore.

Made in the USA
Middletown, DE
23 August 2022

71286389R00116